Popular Mechanics

Scroll Saw Fundamentals

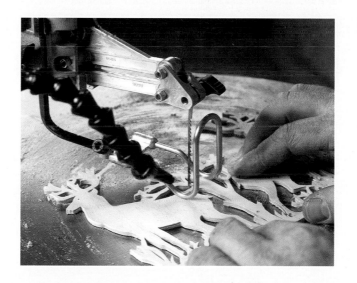

Rick Peters

Hearst Books

A Division of Sterling Publishing Co., Inc.

New York

Production Staff

Produced by How-2 Media Inc.

Design: Triad Design Group

Cover Design: Celia Fuller

Photography: Christopher J. Vendetta

Contributing Writer: Cheryl A. Romano

Cover Photo: Christopher J. Vendetta

Illustrations: Triad Design Group

Copy Editor: Barbara McIntosh Webb

Page Layout: Triad Design Group

Index: Nan Badgett

Library of Congress Cataloging-in-Publication Data
Peters, Rick.
    Popular mechanics workshop. Scroll saw fundamentals :
the complete guide / Rick Peters.
        p. cm.
    Includes index.
    ISBN 1-58816-366-0
    1. Jig saws 2. Woodwork--Patterns. I. Popular mechanics
(Chicago, Ill. : 1959) II. Title.

    TT186.P462 2005
    745.51'3--dc22

                                                    2004054185

10 9 8 7 6 5 4 3 2

Published by Hearst Books
A Division of Sterling Publishing Co., Inc.
387 Park Avenue South, New York, NY 10016

Popular Mechanics is a trademark owned by Hearst Magazines
Property, Inc., in USA, and Hearst Communications, Inc., in
Canada. Hearst Books is a trademark owned by Hearst
Communications, Inc.

www.popularmechanics.com

Distributed in Canada by Sterling Publishing
C/o Canadian Manda Group, 165 Dufferin Street
Toronto, Ontario, Canada M6K 3H6

Distributed in Australia by Capricorn Link (Australia) Pty. Ltd.
P.O. Box 704, Windsor, NSW 2756 Australia

Manufactured in China

ISBN 1-58816-366-0

Copyright © 2005 by Rick Peters

Every effort has been made to ensure that all the information in
this book is accurate. However, due to differing conditions, tools,
and individual skills, the publisher cannot be responsible for any
injuries, losses, and/or other damages that may result from the
use of the information in this book.

Note: The safety guards were removed for clarity in many of the
photographs in this book. Make sure to always use all safety
devices according to the manufacturers' instructions.

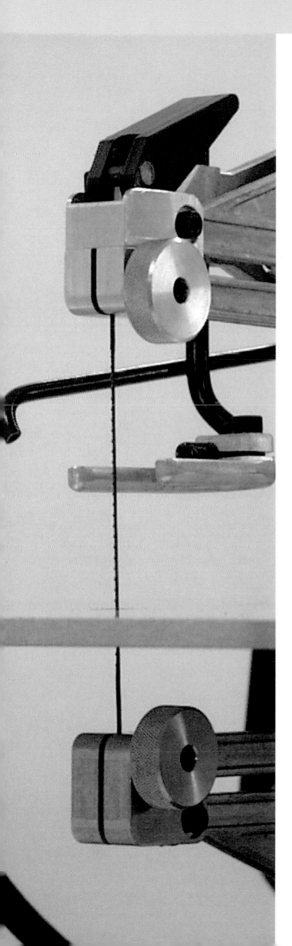

Contents

ACKNOWLEDGMENTS

For all their help, advice, and support, I offer thanks to:

Charles Olson with the Olson Saw Company for supplying photos, technical information, and their top-of-the-line scroll saw blades and accessories.

Hans Derke with Advanced Machinery for supplying photos, technical data, and the high-quality Hegner scroll saw.

Jane VanBergen with Ryobi Tools for supplying photos, technical information, and their bench-top scroll saw.

Robb Murry with R.B. Industries for supplying photos, technical information, and their well-crafted Hawk scroll saw.

Andrea Ash and Jason Feldner at Bosch Power Tools/Dremel for providing technical information, photos, and their well-designed bench-top scroll saw.

Chad Corley with Delta for supplying photos, technical information, and their excellent bench-top scroll saw.

David Olsen with Black & Decker for supplying images and technical information on their bench-top scroll saw.

Henry Raab for DeWalt Tools for providing images, technical information, and their well-thought-out bench-top scroll saw.

Ernie Mellon of Eclipse Saws for providing technical information and photos of the unique Eclipse scroll saw.

The following companies also provided photos for use in this book:

Rexon
Seyco

Special thanks also to:

Christopher Vendetta, ace photographer, for taking great photos in less-than-desirable conditions (my dusty workshop).

Rob Lembo and the staff at Triad Design Group, for their superb illustrations and page layout talents that are evident in every page of this book.

Barb Webb, copyediting whiz, for ferreting out mistakes and gently suggesting corrections.

Heartfelt thanks to my constant inspiration: Cheryl, Lynne, Will, and Beth, for putting up with the craziness that goes with writing a book and living with a woodworker: late nights, wood everywhere, noise from the shop, and sawdust footprints in the house.

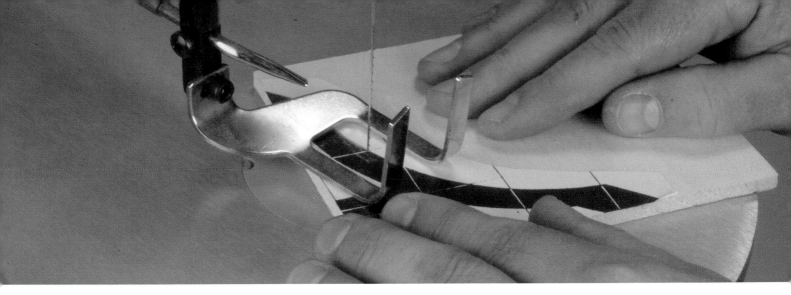

INTRODUCTION

Many woodworkers think a scroll saw is good only for cutting fussy designs in thin wood. They're wrong. Sure, you can cut amazingly intricate curves and details with a scroll saw. But did you know that you can cut dovetail joints on the scroll saw? That it's capable of coping intricate molding? Or that you can use a technique called stack-cutting to duplicate parts with ease? Even the least expensive bench-top scroll saw can tackle these projects and a whole lot more.

And let's get the thin wood myth out of the way: Most scroll saws (even the bench-top models) can handle stock up to 2" in thickness. What's more, the scroll saw can do things no other power tool can do. In particular, a scroll saw is capable of making pierced cuts—that is, cutting inside the perimeter of a workpiece without cutting into its edge. The only other power tool that's remotely capable of this is a handheld jigsaw. And even the smallest blade on one of these can't compete with the almost threadlike blades that a scroll saw will accept. Small blades with many fine teeth mean you can make on-the-spot turns and leave a smooth edge. Yep—on-the-spot turns, where you virtually spin the workpiece and then keep on cutting. Try that with a jigsaw sometime.

In this book, we'll start by taking you through the various types of scroll saws available and show you what to look for—and what to look out for—whether you're buying your first or upgrading to another. Next, we'll walk you through the many blades and accessories available to make your scroll saw even more versatile. Following this is a chapter of easy-to-make jigs for your scroll saw. Then to keep your new or old scroll saw running at peak performance, there's an entire chapter devoted to maintenance: from cleaning and lubricating the arms to modifying blades for special cuts. The final chapter is devoted to projects you can build that showcase a variety of techniques described in the book. We're sure you'll want to hurry off to the shop after you've paged through this book.

Enjoy your woodworking, and make sure to always follow all tool manufacturers' safety warnings.

—James Meigs
Editor-in-Chief, Popular Mechanics

1 Choosing a Scroll Saw

If you're a scroll saw user, chances are good that you're either a woodworker or a scrolling enthusiast. These two groups certainly aren't mutually exclusive, but you'll usually find one or the other. The woodworker uses a scroll saw occasionally to add a decorative detail to a project, or to make a cut that no other power tool in the shop can handle, like a pierced cut (a cut that's made in from the edge of a workpiece). A scrolling enthusiast is someone who has learned what a scroll saw is capable of and often pushes one to its limits. If you're among this select group, you may often design projects around the scroll saw—and these projects may call for no other power tool at all.

With over three dozen different scroll saws to choose from, it's important to identify what you want to do with the saw—and how all these saws differ. That's what this chapter is about. We'll take you through the various types of saws and show you what to look for. Additionally, we'll review features such as motor and table size, fit and finish, and finally, ergonomics. Armed with this information, you'll be able to choose a saw that meets your needs—either as a woodworker, as a scrolling enthusiast, or both.

There are many types and sizes of scroll saws available, everything from large floor-model saws to diminutive bench-top models. Pricing ranges from under $150 to well over $1,000.

Types of Scroll Saws

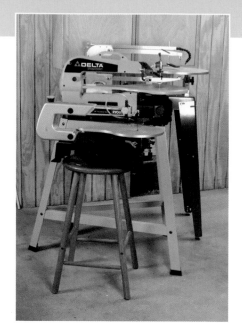

When you shop for almost any stationary power tool, you're looking mainly at power and capacities. Sure, extra features are nice, and ergonomics count; but most tool-buying decisions come done to power, performance, and price. For example, say you're looking to buy a table saw. You're not faced with choosing among five different types. You might be torn between a $1^{1}/_{2}$-hp contractor's saw and a 3-hp cabinet saw, but the saws are similar.

That's what makes choosing a scroll saw a bit of a challenge—there are five different types to choose from. Although scroll saws are typically classified by the depths of their throats—and therefore by their maximum cutting capacity—the way in which the blade is tensioned will have a huge impact on performance. And, since most scrolling is done on thin stock, power isn't as significant. That's why it's important to understand the five tensioning systems: rigid-arm, C-arm, parallel-arm, double-parallel link, and oscillating-loop. For more on the different tensioning systems, see pages 9–13.

Once you've decided on a tensioning system, you can start looking at capacities. You'll need to know things like, how deep is the throat? What's the thickest stock that it can cut at 0 degrees? At 45 degrees? For more on scroll saw capacities, see page 14. Also, the motor type and size are important. Can you get by with one or two speeds, or do you need continuously variable speed? See page 15 for more on motors and speed choices. Finally, what kind of blades the saw can accept—pin or plain end—and how the blades are held in place and tensioned are other major concerns, since you'll be changing and tensioning blades frequently. For more on this, see pages 16–17.

Once you've narrowed down your choices, you can begin to look at features and ergonomics, such as built-in dust collection, where the controls are located, and how easy they are to use. For more on what to look for here, see pages 18–23.

BENCH-TOP VERSUS FLOOR MODEL

With most stationary power tools, there's a clear distinction between bench-top and floor-model tools. Typically, the bench-top tool is smaller, lighter, and less powerful than the floor model; the floor model is big, heavy, and usually a lot more powerful. With bench-top (far saw in photo at left) and floor-model scroll saws (near saw in photo at left), the differences are not as clear. That's because virtually all scroll saws can be used on a bench top. And the only thing that differentiates a floor-model saw from a bench-top is that it has a stand. True, some floor-model scroll saws are in fact larger, heavier, and more powerful than most bench-top models, but this is the case only for a few. Although most bench-top scroll saws have an optional stand, floor models always come with one. You have to ask yourself whether the stand justifies the higher price tag of a floor model.

Rigid-Arm Scroll Saws

For roughly 60 years, the only scroll saw you'd find was a rigid-arm or strained saw, see the top photo. Many woodworkers learned how to scroll-saw on one of these in their childhood shop classes. Rigid-arm scroll saws became all but extinct after the introduction of parallel-arm saws in the early 1980s. Rigid-arm saws can be clearly identified by the fixed or rigid arm that runs from the base around and up over the table, see the left drawing. The arm on quality saws was cast iron for added strength. The motor was heavy-duty and connected to the drive system via a belt. This made for a very heavy unit overall that did a good job of dampening vibration.

Rigid arm blade tensioning

Tension is applied to the blade by a spring inside a housing that attaches to the overhead arm, see the drawing below. The bottom of the blade hooks into a clamp under the table that connects to a drive link. This link attaches to a wheel or pulley connected to the motor. In use, the wheel turns and the drive link pulls the blade down; the spring pulls it back up and keeps tension on the blade. Although this does produce a vertical stroke, the blade tension varies from tight at the bottom of the stroke to light at the top when the spring is compressed. This is a problem especially when using fine blades, which tend to break easily when tension varies during a cut.

ANATOMY OF A RIGID-ARM SAW

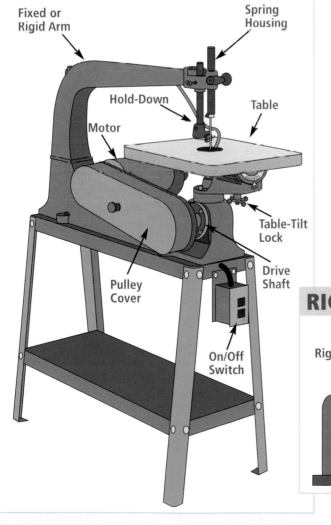

Fixed or Rigid Arm

Spring Housing

Hold-Down

Table

Motor

Pulley Cover

Drive Shaft

Table-Tilt Lock

On/Off Switch

RIGID-ARM BLADE ACTION

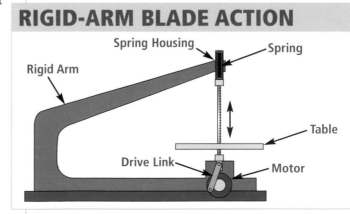

Spring Housing

Spring

Rigid Arm

Table

Drive Link

Motor

C-Arm Scroll Saws

Just like rigid-arm scroll saws, C-arm saws are increasingly hard to find. C-arm scroll saws can be identified by a single arm shaped like a "C" as shown in the top drawing. Although these saws do a better job of tensioning the blade than a rigid arm saw, they don't provide true vertical scrolling; see below.

Anatomy of a C-arm saw
What really sets a C-arm saw apart from the others is that it has only a single pivot point. If you look at the closed portion of the C-arm, you'll usually find a pivot bearing and an arm support bracket, as shown in the top drawing. The arm is forced to oscillate by the drive link attached to the drive wheel, as shown in the bottom drawing.

C-arm blade tensioning
A blade is clamped between the pads attached to the ends of the C. Tension is controlled by a knob that connects to the upper arm of the C. As noted earlier, this type of saw does apply constant tension to the blade. The problem is that the pivoting action of the C-arm creates a stroke that is not truly vertical, as shown in the bottom drawing. On the plus side, this "reciprocating"-type blade action makes for a very aggressive cut. As a result, these saws are still often used in production environments where highly detailed work is not needed.

ANATOMY OF A C-ARM SCROLL SAW

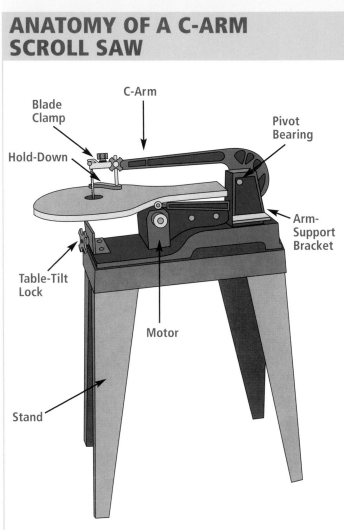

C-ARM BLADE ACTION

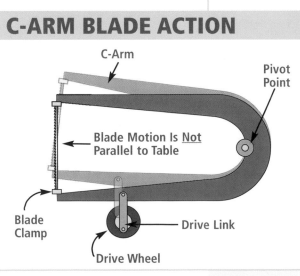

Parallel-Arm Scroll Saws

Although the concept of the parallel-arm scroll saw has been around for over a century, it wasn't until the German toolmaker Hegner re-engineered and upgraded the saw in the early 1980s that it became the most common type of scroll saw available. Unlike the C-arm saw, which has only a single pivot point, a parallel-arm saw has two. Big deal, you say? Well, it is a big deal because this type of saw produces a true vertical stroke where the blade is under constant, uniform tension. And that's what a scroller needs to make detailed, delicate cuts. That's why 80% of the scroll saws listed in the charts on pages 24–25 are parallel-arm saws.

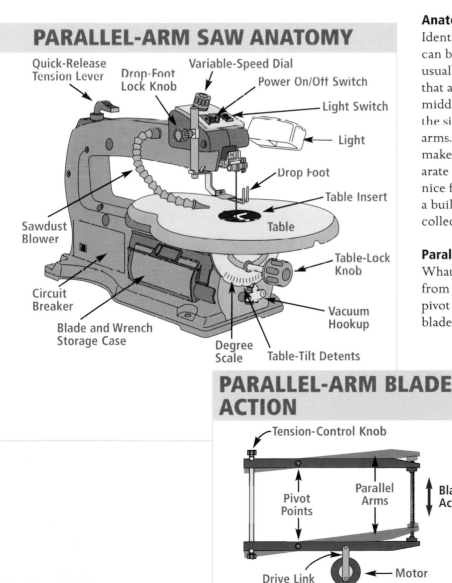

PARALLEL-ARM SAW ANATOMY

- Quick-Release Tension Lever
- Drop-Foot Lock Knob
- Variable-Speed Dial
- Power On/Off Switch
- Light Switch
- Light
- Drop Foot
- Table Insert
- Table
- Sawdust Blower
- Table-Lock Knob
- Circuit Breaker
- Vacuum Hookup
- Blade and Wrench Storage Case
- Degree Scale
- Table-Tilt Detents

PARALLEL-ARM BLADE ACTION

- Tension-Control Knob
- Pivot Points
- Parallel Arms
- Blade Action
- Drive Link
- Motor

Anatomy of a parallel-arm saw

Identifying a parallel-arm saw by sight can be tricky. That's because the arms are usually obscured by the sides of the saw that attach to the base, as shown in the middle drawing. It isn't until you remove the sides that you can see the two parallel arms. Because most tool manufacturers make parallel-arm saws, each tries to separate their saw from the pack by adding nice features such as a built-in blower, a built-in light, a vacuum port or dust-collection box, and even blade storage.

Parallel-arm blade tensioning

What distinguishes a parallel-arm saw from the rest is that each arm has its own pivot point, see the bottom drawing. The blade attaches to clamps in the front of the arms, and the ends are usually joined by a tensioning system. When the drive link attached to the motor forces the bottom arm up and down, it pulls the upper arm with it, creating a true vertical blade stroke, dampening vibration. This was a plus, since the machine was prone to vibration because of the blade-tensioning system.

Double-Parallel Link Saws

The next step up the evolutionary chain from a parallel-arm saw is the double-parallel link scroll saw, as shown in the top photo. Although this type of saw has a complex tensioning and drive system, it does create an almost vibration-free cut. Because the tensioning and drive system is so complex, double-parallel link saws are more expensive than their simpler parallel-arm cousins.

Double-parallel link anatomy

As with a parallel-arm saw, you can't identify a double-parallel link saw by sight—you need to remove the side covers to see what's going on inside. Even though these saws run smoother than parallel-arm saws, manufacturers still add features which scrollers have come to expect in a quality saw, like a built-in light and blower, along with accessible controls and variable speed (see the middle drawing).

Double-parallel link tensioning

The bottom drawing is a simplified version of the double-parallel link tensioning system. Instead of two pivot points like a parallel-arm saw, a double-parallel link saw has four. Here's how the blade ends up going up and down: The motor drives a vertical rocker back and forth via a connecting rod. The vertical rocker forces a pair of horizontal links to go back and forth, which forces the top and bottom rocker assemblies to pivot and move the blade up and down. The major disadvantage to this saw type is that when a blade breaks, it will continue to reciprocate until the saw is turned off.

DOUBLE-PARALLEL LINK SAW ANATOMY

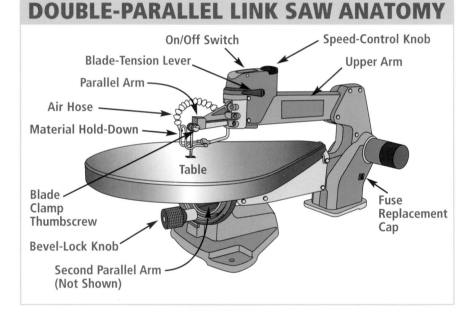

On/Off Switch
Speed-Control Knob
Blade-Tension Lever
Upper Arm
Parallel Arm
Air Hose
Material Hold-Down
Table
Blade Clamp Thumbscrew
Bevel-Lock Knob
Second Parallel Arm (Not Shown)
Fuse Replacement Cap

DOUBLE-PARALLEL LINK BLADE ACTION

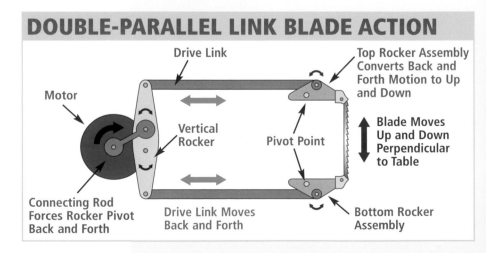

Drive Link
Top Rocker Assembly Converts Back and Forth Motion to Up and Down
Motor
Vertical Rocker
Pivot Point
Blade Moves Up and Down Perpendicular to Table
Connecting Rod Forces Rocker Pivot Back and Forth
Drive Link Moves Back and Forth
Bottom Rocker Assembly

Oscillating-Loop Saws

The Eclipse saw (top photo) is currently the only oscillating-loop saw on the market; it was developed by Ernie Mellon, who chose a toothed belt to drive the blade and apply tension to it. The belt or loop moves back and forth (oscillates) to force the blade up and down. Of all the blade-tensioning and drive systems discussed, the oscillating-loop saw produces the truest vertical stroke.

Anatomy of an oscillating-loop saw

It's simple to identify an oscillating-loop saw because there's currently only one manufacturer—Eclipse. It's easily identified by its large frame with enclosed sides, as shown in the middle drawing. Controls are easily accessible, and the large, flat table provides an excellent platform for scrolling.

Oscillating-loop blade tensioning

If you were to remove the side covers of the Eclipse, inside you'd see a drive system like the one illustrated in the bottom drawing. A motor drives an arm, which attaches to a toothed rocker. This rocker pivots back and forth to drive the belt that runs up over a set of pulleys to the blade clamps holding the blade. As the belt oscillates back and forth, the blade moves up and down in a perfect vertical stroke, which makes it ideal for delicate, ornate scrolling.

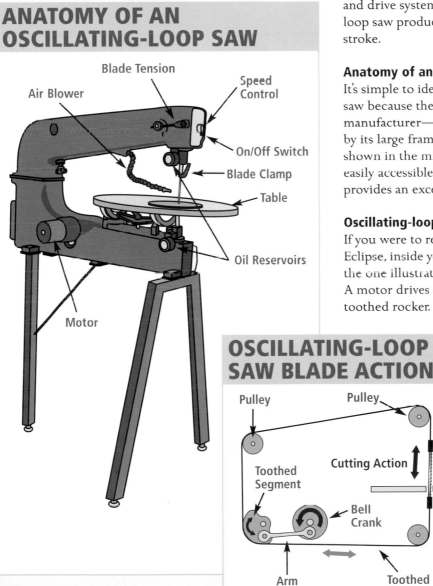

ANATOMY OF AN OSCILLATING-LOOP SAW

- Blade Tension
- Air Blower
- Speed Control
- On/Off Switch
- Blade Clamp
- Table
- Oil Reservoirs
- Motor

OSCILLATING-LOOP SAW BLADE ACTION

- Pulley
- Pulley
- Cutting Action
- Toothed Segment
- Bell Crank
- Table
- Arm
- Toothed Belt

Cutting Capacity

When choosing a scroll saw, you should give some thought to the cutting capacity of the saw—in particular, the saw's throat depth and its maximum thickness capacity.

Throat depth

The throat depth of a scroll saw refers to the distance from the blade to the back of the saw frame, as illustrated in the top drawing. This will limit how far you can cut into a workpiece. For instance, if the saw you're interested in has a 16" throat depth, you can cut to the center of a 32" square panel. If you need increased ripping capacity (to rip a 48"-long 1×6 in half, for example), you can get around the throat-depth limitation by modifying the blade; see page 157 for more on this.

Thickness capacity

Another capacity that you may or may not find limiting is the maximum thickness cut—how thick a board you can cut on the saw. This number is typically given with the blade completely vertical, as shown in the middle photo. It's common to find a 2" thickness capacity on most scroll saws. And it's important to note that this capacity is usually halved when the table is tilted to 45 degrees.

Table size

Although the size of the saw's table doesn't directly affect its cutting capacities, it does affect how easily the saw can handle larger workpieces. Common table dimensions are width and depth, along with tongue dimensions (if applicable), as illustrated in the bottom drawing. The larger the table, the better it will support big work. On the flip side, since much scrollwork is relatively small, an overlarge table with a blade near its middle can make it difficult to reach in when scrolling smaller pieces.

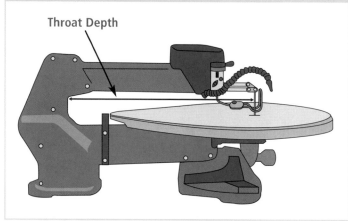

THROAT DEPTH

Throat Depth

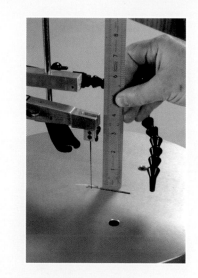

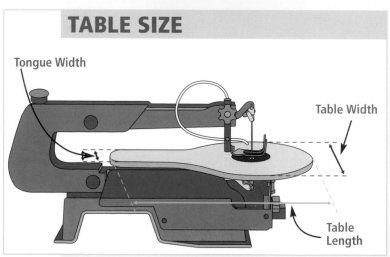

TABLE SIZE

Tongue Width

Table Width

Table Length

Scroll Saw Motors

As we mentioned earlier in the chapter, the motor on a scroll saw isn't as important as it is on other stationary power tools because much of the scrolling you'll do will be in thin stock. Motor

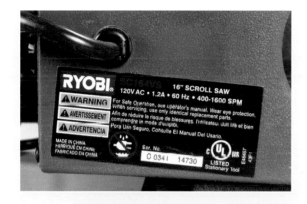

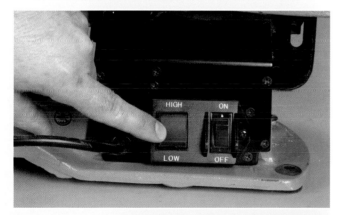

power is really a factor only if you intend to cut stock well over 1" thick. What may be more important to you are the speeds that are available.

Motor power

The best all-around indicator of a saw's ability to power through stock is its amperage rating. An amperage rating is usually clearly displayed on the saw's label—often on or near the motor, as shown in the top photo. As a general rule of thumb, the higher the amperage, the more powerful the motor. Something to watch out for are horsepower ratings, particularly when a description says that a saw "develops" a certain amount of horsepower. That's because no motor produces usable horsepower unless it is slowed down by applying a mechanical load. "Developed horsepower" may be 2 to 5 times the continuous-duty rating of a motor. A term like "develops 3 hp" is meaningless marketing hype—stick with the amperage rating.

Speed options

Scroll saws are available with a single speed, dual speeds (middle photo), three to five speeds, and continuously variable over a certain range (bottom photo). Typical variable-speed saws offer ranges from around 400 strokes per minute up to around 1700 strokes per minute. Other saws offer a low end of zero strokes per minute up to a maximum of 2000 strokes per minute.

In most cases where you'll be cutting wood, you'll want to use the highest speed the saw is capable of to get the smoothest cut. You'll need slower speeds only when cutting materials other than wood and when cutting particularly fragile stock like veneer. If you plan to exclusively scroll wood, a single-speed saw will most likely be all you'll need. If, however, you intend to scroll plastics, metal, or veneer, choose a saw with variable speeds. In most cases a saw with three or four ranges will work just fine. Continuously variable speeds aren't necessary; many scrollers leave their saws on max speed and rarely, if ever, adjust the speed.

Blade-Clamp Mechanisms

How easy or difficult it is to change a blade will depend primarily on the type of clamp mechanisms the saw employs. This detail can have a profound impact on your scrolling. That's because you'll be changing or removing blades about as frequently as you change the bits on a drill. Sure, you'll need to replace a blade if it breaks; but more importantly, you'll be changing blades frequently to get the best cut. And if you're making pierced cuts—extremely common in scrollwork—you'll need to release one end of the blade, thread it through the workpiece, and re-clamp it in place. There are two basic types of mechanisms: screw clamps and quick-release clamps.

Screw clamps

For many years, the only way to change a blade on a scroll saw was to reach for a special wrench like the one shown in the top photo. This rather cumbersome method was often frustrating. Even with aids to hold the small screw-clamp heads in place while you removed and inserted blades, it could drive even the most patient woodworker over the edge.

Quick-release clamps

The introduction of the quick-release clamp was a boon to frustrated scrollers everywhere. With this type of clamp, the blade is pinched between two pads and locked in place with a lever, as shown in the middle photo. With no tools required, changing blades isn't a chore. To handle the varying thicknesses of blades, the distance between the pads—and therefore the pressure they exert—is adjustable with a nut on the side of the clamp. Quick-release clamps make pierced scrollwork less of a chore and more fun.

TABLE INSERTS

The type of table insert you use will also affect how easy or difficult it is to change blades. Standard inserts (right in photo) are slotted to let the top portion of the blade move about, to make it easy to change and thread through a workpiece. A zero-clearance insert (left in photo) fully supports the workpiece but makes blade changes more challenging.

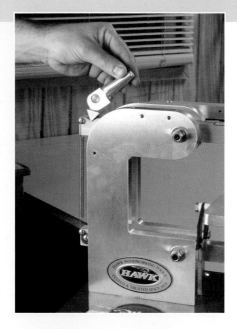

Blade Tensioning

If the blade-clamping system (page 16) of a scroll saw is a big deal, so is the way that tension is applied to the blade. Every time you change a blade or need to release the clamps in order to thread a blade through a workpiece, you have to first release the tension, and then re-tension the blade once it's in place.

Cam action

A common way to release and tension the blade is with a cam, like the one shown in the top photo. The cam threads onto a rod that hooks into a spring. This spring stretches between the ends of the arms opposite the blade. You flip the cam up to release the tension and press it down to apply it. Rotating the cam increases or decreases the amount of tension by raising or lowering the spring. With practice, you'll learn at what "o'clock" position the cam is in to properly tension various-sized blades.

Knob-tensioned

On some saws, tension is adjusted via a knob on the back of the saw. Just like the cam action, the knob attaches to a rod that controls the length of a spring (middle photo). Tension is typically released separately via a quick-release lever located on top of the arm positioned over the blade. This is not as convenient as the cam action system because two separate controls are needed to release and adjust tension. Additionally, a knob makes it harder to identify tension positions for blade sizes.

Tension and release in one

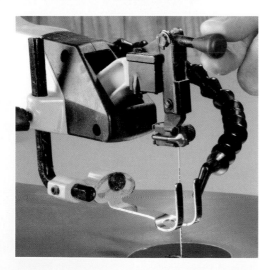

One of the better blade-tension systems was developed by Delta. This system incorporates the release and the tension adjustment in a unique adjustable lever, see the bottom photo. Toggling the lever releases and tensions the blade. Twisting the knob on the end of the lever adjusts tension. Here again, a knob makes it difficult to identify tension positions for blade sizes, but it's a small trade-off for having all the tension controls up front and fully accessible at all times.

Dust Blowers

For the most part, scroll saws don't generate a lot of dust. You'll rarely see one hooked up to a shop dust collection system. But they do create dust—it's a fine dust—and it usually ends up right where you don't want it: on your pattern lines. That's why virtually every scroll saw has a built-in blower. This is usually nothing more than a rubber diaphragm that compresses like a bellows every time the blade goes up and down. Tubing connects the diaphragm to a metal or plastic arm that directs the airflow down onto the workpiece to blow away dust. These arms may be either fixed or adjustable.

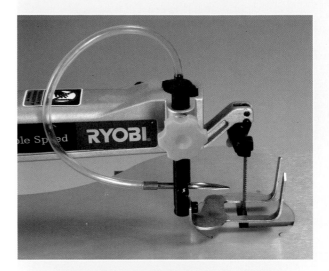

Fixed arms

Fixed arms, like the one shown in the top photo, typically attach to the post used for the hold-down mechanism and blade guard. Although they usually work fairly well, you may often wish they were adjustable. You can, with care, bend a metal arm slightly if needed; however, over time you risk the possibility of snapping it off.

Adjustable arms

A fairly recent innovation in blowers is to replace the fixed arms with fully articulated arms, like the one shown in the middle photo. Not only are these adjustable over a wide range, but also the friction-tight articulated sections hold the arm in place exactly where you position it. Within a few years, you'll likely see these as standard on all new saws.

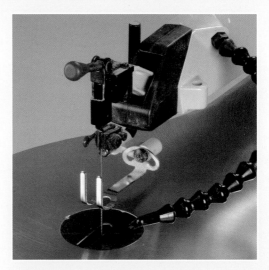

Add-on systems

If you have an older scroll saw that didn't come with a built-in blower, or you're dissatisfied with your current blower setup, you can purchase an add-on blower kit like the one shown in the bottom photo. These usually consist of an articulated arm, tubing, and plastic cable clamps to attach the tubing to your saw. Air power is supplied by a blower that you buy separately—the kind used for home aquariums work great for this. For more on how to add a blower to your saw, see page 152.

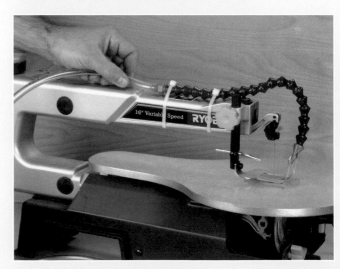

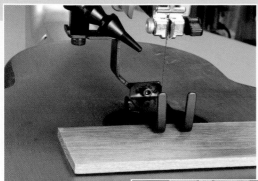

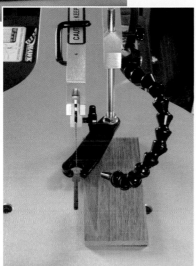

Hold-Downs & Blade Guards

Along with blade-clamping and tensioning systems, you'll find you need to adjust the hold-downs and blade guards on your saw every time you change or release a blade. Hold-downs are designed to press the workpiece down flat against the saw's table. This prevents the blade from lifting the workpiece up during a cut, which helps produce accurate cuts and reduces chatter. A blade guard is designed to keep your fingers from contacting the blade. It really should be called a finger guard; after all, it's not the blade you're guarding—it's your fingers.

On most saws, the hold-down and blade guard consist of a single unit and can't be adjusted independently. Because of this, the functionality of one or the other must suffer. The blade guard is the one that you'll usually find lacking—it often gets in the way of your cut, see below.

Hold-downs

There are two basic types of hold-downs you'll find on scroll saws: a dual-pronged metal hold-down (top left photo) and a flexible rubber hold-down that's notched to fit around the blade (top right photo). For pressing the workpiece into the saw table, the dual-pronged hold-down tends to work better, as it offers two contact points. The disadvantage is that it can be touchier to adjust and can often cause the workpiece to bind.

Blade guards

Just like hold-downs, blade guards come in similar types: the dual-pronged metal style (bottom right photo) and a single bar that either fits around the blade or has a vertical post to keep your fingers away from the blade (bottom left photo). The dual-pronged guard offers the more unobstructed view of the blade, but also allows a finger to pass between the prongs. The post-style guard blocks the blade well from the front, but doesn't offer much protection from the side. Neither is foolproof; it's up to the operator to keep fingers away from the blade.

Saw Tables

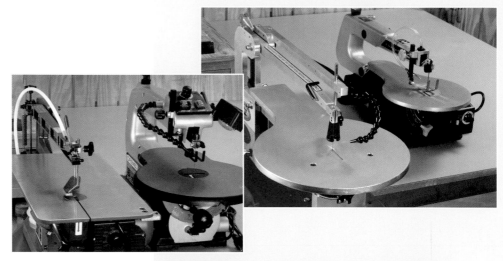

As you sift through the myriad scroll saws to look for the one that's perfect for your needs, you'll want to take a look at the table top. Because much scrollwork is detailed, odds are you'll be spending considerable time with your hands on the table. How comfortable this is depends on the size and shape of the top, what it's made of, and how it tilts for angled cuts.

Size and shape

The size of a scroll saw's table will have an impact on the size of workpieces you can comfortably handle (top right photo). A larger top makes it easy to tackle larger projects. Small tops offer less support but are generally more comfortable to use when scrolling small parts. The table's shape also contributes to support. Square tables (like the left saw in the top left photo) offer more support over a greater area than round tables. Even so, some scrollers prefer a round table; they find it more comfortable to spin a workpiece for an on-the-spot turn versus a square table, where it's possible to catch their arms on the corners.

Table-top material

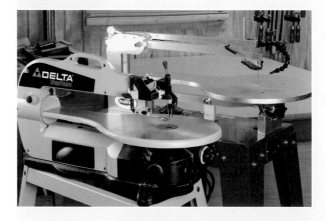

You'll also have to choose between table-top materials: cast iron or aluminum (see the middle photo). Cast iron is heavy and helps dampen vibration, but it will rust and requires maintenance. An aluminum top doesn't rust, but it won't be as heavy as cast iron and so can't dampen vibration as well. You'll often find aluminum tops on premium scroll saws where the manufacturer has built a close-tolerance machine with vibration practically engineered out of the unit. In this case, the aluminum top is ideal: no rust, no vibration.

TABLE TILT

One way only Most scroll saws tilt in one direction only, usually to the left. This is fine for most work but can be limiting when it comes to joinery, intarsia, and marquetry work.

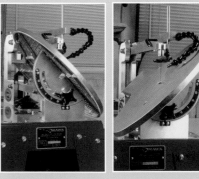

Both ways Whenever possible, choose a saw whose table tilts both ways. The table on the RBI Hawk saw shown here tilts 45 degrees both ways, so you can tackle any angled scrolling task.

Fit and Finish

As you search for the perfect scroll saw, you'll probably detect major differences in the fit and finish of the saws you inspect—how well the parts fit together and whether or not they operate smoothly. Along with this is the issue of how the parts of the saw are

machined. Are they smooth or rough? And does it matter? The answer to this question depends on the part and its function. If, for example, the sides of the base casting are rough, it really doesn't matter because the base is just the foundation for the saw. It adds weight and supports the critical parts.

Check the top

The fit and finish of moving parts and the top are another matter entirely. These need to be well-machined—not just smooth. A top that's smooth but warped is useless. When shopping for a saw in person, it's always a good idea to take a metal straightedge with you to the store. This way, you can set it on edge across the table top and check for flatness. If you see any gap at all between the top and the straightedge, consider another saw. Yes, you can have a top flattened at a local machine shop, but at considerable expense.

Inspect the castings

When inspecting a saw, check out the casting of the parts that move or are detachable. For instance, lift out the table insert and carefully feel the inside edges of the inset with your finger as shown in the middle photo. They'll likely be rough and that's okay; you can file this smooth (see page 149). But little things like this can hint at the overall quality of a saw. If you find it smooth inside, you'll know that the manufacturer has taken extra time and care to machine it smooth, which speaks well for the overall condition of the saw.

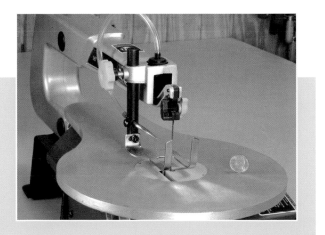

QUICK VIBRATION TEST

Looking for a quick dynamic test of a saw's overall quality? Set a nickel on edge on the saw's top and turn on the saw. On a well-engineered unit, the saw will run smoothly and the nickel will stay on edge. On a poorly designed saw, machine vibration will tip the nickel over.

Ergonomics

Once you've narrowed down the field and are starting to get serious about a saw or two, the best thing you can do is to get your hands on the saws in question. Most home centers carry a variety of scroll saws that you can check out. Alternatively, one of the best ways to preview different saws is to go to a woodworking show near you. Not only will you find the major brands fairly well represented, but you're also likely to find many of the premium scroll saw manufacturers on hand, too.

There really is no substitute for sitting down and actually cutting on a saw. If this isn't possible, just operating the controls with the power off can give you an idea of how well the saw may fit your needs. Take the time to locate and operate the following: power switch, speed control (if applicable), table tilt, and blade-changing controls.

Power switch

Since you turn off a saw every time you change a blade or stop to make a pierced cut, the location of the power switch and the ease with which it's toggled on and off will affect how comfortable the saw is to use. Both switches in the saws in the top photo are readily accessible. Left-handers may find the saw with the top-mounted switch at right in the photo easier to reach with their left hand than the right-side-mounted switch of the saw at left.

Speed control

The location and operation of the speed control are not as important as those of the power switch because most scrollers don't adjust the speed often. Even so, it's nice to have convenient controls. The rear saw in the middle photo has a more accessible top-mounted control than the side-mounted control of the near saw.

Table tilt

Most table-tilt controls are located under the saw table and are easy to reach. The angle indicators may

be different, however. On most saws, the indicator is located near the angle lock (left saw in bottom photo). Other saws locate the indicator toward the rear of the table (right saw in bottom photo). Which works best for you is a matter of personal preference.

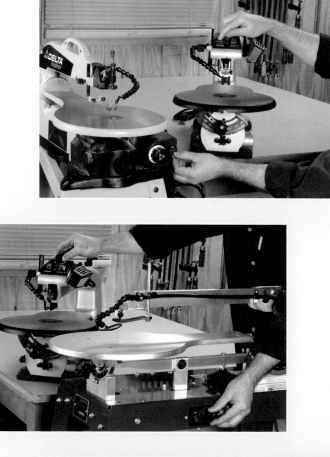

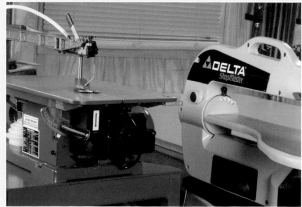

Changing Blades

This chapter has stressed the importance of a saw's blade-changing mechanism because it has a great impact on how easy or difficult the saw is to use. A quick-release-type clamping system is the recommended type, as it allows for hassle-free blade changes. Although many saws now come with a quick-release-style clamp on the upper arm (top photo), most do not have a quick-release clamp on the lower arm (middle photo).

Granted, you'll need to release the upper clamp more often than the bottom because you only need to release one end of the blade to thread it through a workpiece when making a pierced cut. But a lower arm that doesn't have a quick-release clamp makes it tougher to change or replace a blade—which is also something you'll be doing often. Whenever possible, pick a saw with dual quick-release clamps, as shown in the middle photo. You'll be glad you did.

Tensioning controls

The final ergonomic feature to look at is how the blade tension is adjusted. Many saws have separate release and tension adjustment controls. Those saws with controls near the rear of the saw, such as the far saw in the bottom photo, make it necessary to get up and walk around to the back of the saw to make an adjustment. Saws that provide for up-front release and tensioning adjustments, like the front saw in the bottom photo, don't require movement, as the controls are at the scroller's fingertips.

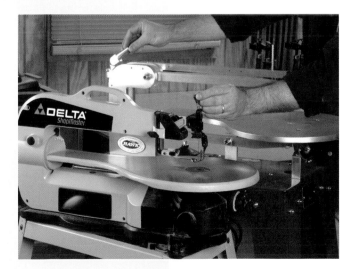

■ RECOMMENDATIONS

If you're just getting started in scrolling, a bench-top scroll saw is your best choice. There are a number of inexpensive saws available that you can experiment on to see whether scrolling is for you (see the chart on the opposite page). The saws made by Dremel offer good value for the money and they have well-thought-out controls. Delta makes excellent-quality bench-top scroll saws that come with dual quick-release blade clamps for hassle-free blade changes. As mentioned earlier, it really is best if you can get your hands on the saws that you're interested in. A saw that's perfect for one woodworker may be a bad fit for another, purely because of ergonomics.

If you've been scrolling for a while and have pushed a bench-top saw to its limits, it's probably time to step up to a premium floor-model saw. The RBI Hawk, Hegner, and Excalibur saws are well worth the investment. They are all capable of near vibration-free cuts, which allows for intricate, detailed cuts even in fragile or hard-to-cut woods. Most of these saws have pretty stiff price tags (usually over $1,000), so be sure to research thoroughly before making a purchase. Don't take someone else's word—go to a woodworking store or show where these saws are displayed so you can get your hands on them to see which one fits your needs the best.

It's also important to note that a scroll saw may accept only one type of blade—pin-end or plain-end. Other saws accept both and, given the choice between two similar saws, pick the one that accepts both types; you never know when you might need that versatility. For more on these two types of blades and how each can affect your scrolling, see page 28 in Chapter 2.

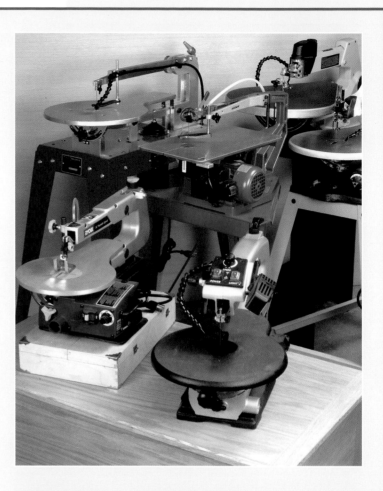

SCROLLSAW ASSOCIATION OF THE WORLD

If you'd like to learn what other scrollers think about their scroll saws, why not ask? The Scrollsaw Association of the World (SAW) has a website devoted to scrolling; they can be found online at www.saw-online.com. Regardless of whether you're just getting started or have been making dust for years, regardless of the brand of saw you own, you'll find something of interest on this website. SAW has members scattered around the world who all share a passion for scrolling. Local chapters of SAW offer meetings, auctions, picnics, and more, all designed to help you gather with like-minded folks to learn more about scrolling.

SCROLL SAW COMPARISON

Brand	Model	Throat	Drive Type	Motor Size	Blade	Speed (strokes per minute)	Table Tilt	Max cut at 0 degrees	Stroke Length	Wt. (lbs.)
Black & Decker	BT4000	16"	PA	1.3 amp	Pin or plain	400–1700	47 left, 2 right	2"	$7/8$"	45
Craftsman	21616	16"	PA	1.0 amp	Pin only	Single 1725	45 left, 0 right	2"	$3/4$"	46
Craftsman	21610	16"	PA	1.4 amp	Pin or plain	400–1600	45 left, 45 right	2"	$7/8$"	53
Craftsman	21620	20"	PA	1.4 amp	Pin or plain	400–1600	45 left, 45 right	$2 1/4$"	$7/8$"	54
Delta	SS350	16"	PA	2 amp	Plain only	600–1650	45 left, 0 right	2"	$3/4$"	60
Delta	SS250	16"	PA	2 amp	Plain only	400–1800	45 left, 0 right	2"	$7/8$"	46.5
Delta	SS200	16"	PA	1.8 amp	Plain only	Single 1750	45 left, 0 right	2"	$7/8$"	40
Delta	P20	20.5"	PA	3.5 amp	Plain only	400–2000*	15 left, 47 right	2"	$7/8$"	115
Dewalt	DW788	20"	PL	1.3 amp	Plain only	400–1750	45 left, 45 right	2"	$3/4$"	56
Dremel	1680	16"	PA	$1/6$ hp	Pin or plain	500–1,600	45 left, 45 right	2"	$3/4$"	40
Eclipse		20"	OL	$1/5$ hp	Plain only	200–1350	45 left, 45 right	$1 1/4$"	$1 1/2$"	90
Excalibur	19	19"	PL	1.4 amp	Plain only	60–1550	45 left, 30 right	2"	$3/4$"	65
Excalibur	30	30"	PL	1.4 amp	Plain only	60–1550	45 left, 30 right	2"	$3/4$"	75
Grizzly	G0536	16"	PA	$1/5$ hp	Pin only	540–1885	30 left	$2 1/8$"	$3/4$"	35
Grizzly	G0537	$21 7/8$"	CA	$1/5$ hp	Pin only	425–1322	30 left	$2 1/8$"	$3/4$"	52
Grizzly	G5776	$15 7/8$"	PA	$1/8$ hp	Pin or plain	400–1400	45 left	$2 1/4$"	$5/8$"	35
Grizzly	G7949	$15 7/8$"	PA	$1/8$ hp	Pin only	Single 1720	45 left	$2 1/4$"	$7/8$"	35
Hegner	Multimax 14E	14"	PA	2.8 amp	Plain only	Single	45 left	2"	$3/4$"	40
Hegner	18	18"	PA	2.8 amp	Plain only	400–1700	45 left, 12 right	$2 3/8$"	$3/4$"	56
Hegner	22	22"	PA	2.8 amp	Plain only	400–1700	45 left, 12 right	$2 3/8$"	$3/4$"	73
Makita	SJ401	16"	PA	1.2 amp	Pin or plain	400–1600	45 left, 15 right	2"	$7/8$"	34
PS Wood	14	14"	PA	1.8 amp	Plain only	1060–1575[†]	45 left, 35 right	$2 1/2$"	1"	65
PS Wood	21	21"	PA	2.2 amp	Plain only	170–1370[‡]	45 left, 35 right	$2 1/2$"	1"	90
RBI Hawk	216VS	16"	PA	2.0 amp	Plain only	300–1725	45 left, 45 right	$2 1/8$"	$7/8$"	73
RBI Hawk	220VS	20"	PA	2.0 amp	Plain only	300–1725	45 left, 45 right	$2 5/8$"	$7/8$"	93
RBI Hawk	226VS	26"	PA	2.0 amp	Plain only	300–1725	45 left, 45 right	$2 5/8$"	$7/8$"	97
Rexon	DTS16A	16"	PA	0.52 amp	Pin or plain	500–1600	45 left, 45 right	2"	$3/4$"	44
Rexon	SS16A	16"	PA	0.48 amp	Pin or plain	900 & 1400	45 left, 0 right	2"	$3/4$"	46
Ryobi	SC164VS	16"	PA	1.2 amp	Pin or plain	400–1600	45 left, 5 right	2"	$3/4$"	28
Ryobi	SC180VS	18"	PA	1.2 amp	Pin or plain	500–1600	45 left, 5 right	2"	$3/4$"	28

Drive type: PA = parallel arm, PL = parallel link, OL = oscillating-loop, CA = C-arm

* six speeds/belt-driven

[†] three speeds: 1060, 1350, and 1575 spm

[‡] five speeds: 170, 450, 790, 1140, and 1370 spm

2 Scroll Saw Accessories

With most other stationary power tools there are dozens of jigs available to help give you precision control—but not with the scroll saw. That's because the nature of scrolling makes this unnecessary. Although some scrollwork requires absolute precision, most of it does not. Sure, you want to follow a pattern line as best you can. But in most cases if you stray from the line a bit and then gradually correct the mistake, it won't affect the overall look of the finished piece. For those times when precision is required, it's up to the skill of the operator to provide it. There's simply no jig that can duplicate the keen eye and steady hand of an accomplished scroller.

What you *will* find in terms of accessories for scroll saws are blades, blades, and more blades. With over eight styles and ten sizes to choose from, this can get confusing. So, the bulk of this chapter is devoted to helping you choose the right blade for the job at hand. There's also information about the non-jig-type accessories you can buy to make your scrolling safe and more enjoyable.

While blades are the number one scroll saw accessory, there are a number of other accessories that can make your scrolling safer, more efficient, and more comfortable. Popular choices are foot pedals to control power to the saw, lights and magnifiers to better see what you're cutting, and kits to upgrade your blade clamps.

Blade Types

Scroll saws accept one of two types of blades—pin-end or plain-end—or both. Most older saws accept pin-end blades only, and many modern saws accept only plain-end blades. The drawing at right illustrates the difference between the two.

Pin-end

On a pin-end blade, a short metal pin runs horizontally through each end of the blade. This setup lets the scroller quickly change blades by simply pushing down on the spring-loaded clip (or pads) that is slotted to accept the blade. Small semi-round depressions in the clip or pads accept the pin so it instantly locks in position. For many years, the only scroll saw blades manufactured had pin ends—and many are still in use today. It's too bad that many of today's scrollers shun pin-end blades, because they're easy to use, are very rugged, and are great for simple scrolling of toys and other projects that don't require intricate details. Pin-end blades are available in different widths, thickness, and teeth per inch (tpi).

Plain-end

Plain-end blades have no pin to hold them in place. This makes them fussier to install and adjust and requires a saw with clamping pads that squeeze together to pinch the blade. This makes for a generally less secure mounting than pin-end and, until recently, required a special wrench to loosen or tighten the pads. But with the advent of quick-release pads, tools are no longer required to change a blade on many saws. Instead, quick-release clamp pads are opened and closed by way of a small lever.

So if a plain-end blade is trickier to install than a pin-end blade, why do so many scrollers prefer plain-end blades? It has to do with access holes—the holes you drill in a workpiece to make pierced cuts. In order for the pin on a pin-end blade to pass through a workpiece, the hole has to be much, much larger. For example, if you compare a pin-end blade and a plain-end blade that have the same number of teeth per inch, you'll see that the pin-end blade needs a $3/16$" hole to pass through. The equivalent plain-end blade, though, can get through a tiny $3/64$" hole. Obviously, if you want to make a series of pierced cuts on a delicate piece of fretwork, you'll want to make the access holes as small as possible so they won't be noticeable. That's the reason for the popularity of plain-end blades.

PIN-END VS. PLAIN-END BLADES

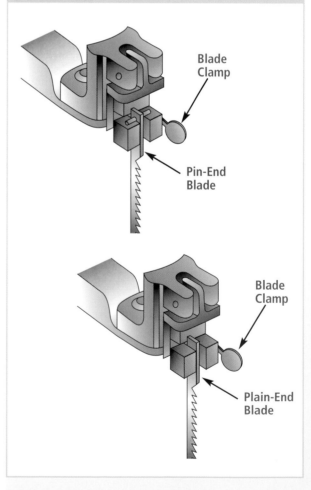

Blade Clamp

Pin-End Blade

Blade Clamp

Plain-End Blade

HOW SCROLL SAW BLADES ARE MADE

Scroll saw blades are manufactured by one of three methods: grinding, punching, or milling. Each has advantages and disadvantages.

Ground blades. The teeth on ground blades are formed by grinding them to shape with a stone wheel. This produces the sharpest edge on all tooth surfaces, and these blades cut the smoothest and straightest. The downside is that they cost more than punched or milled blades.

Punched blades. To provide blade clearance, the teeth on a punched blade are alternately bent or set. Punched blades are generally wider than other manufactured blades and produce a medium-smooth finish.

Milled blades. The teeth on a milled blade are formed by milling cutters similar to those used to make band saw blades. The blade blank is soft steel and is heat-treated after milling to create tough teeth. The milling process does create a slight burr, which can cause a workpiece to "drift" during a cut.

Tooth Configuration

To give you an idea of the variety of scroll saw blades available, consider this: The Olson Saw Company (www.olson.com) makes over 80 different blades in over ten sizes and eight different tooth configurations. Blade lengths available are 3" for hobby saws, and 5" and 6" for bench-top and floor-model saws—the 5" length being the more common. The sizes are fairly easy to deal with; the significant thing that varies is the number of teeth per inch, see page 36 for more on this. How the teeth are configured is more complex, and this is where you need to match up the tooth configuration to what you're doing and the material you're cutting. There are eight basic tooth configurations: standard-tooth, skip-tooth, precision-ground teeth, reverse-tooth, crown-tooth, double-tooth, spiral teeth, and metal-cutting blades; see the chart below and pages 30–35, respectively, for more information on each configuration and what they are optimized for.

COMPARISON OF BLADE TYPES

Blade Type	Application
Crown-tooth	Two-way cutting action affords better control for delicate cuts. Splinter-free cuts in softwoods and hardwoods as well as in plywood. Also excellent for cutting plastic.
Double-tooth	The blade of choice for scrollers wanting excellent control while producing cuts in hardwoods and softwoods with little or no fuzz on the bottom of the workpiece.
Metal-cutting	Designed specifically for cutting metals, these blades can tackle nonferrous metals (aluminum, copper, and brass) as long as the thickness does not exceed 1/8".
Precision-ground-teeth	Milled teeth in pre-hardened steel have no burr and produce incredibly smooth cuts with no drift problems. Available in either skip-tooth or double-tooth configuration.
Reverse-skip-tooth	Identical to skip-tooth blades except the teeth at the bottom end are reversed to prevent splintering on the bottom of a workpiece. Produce exceptionally clean cuts in standard and premium plywoods.
Skip-tooth	Made from soft steel and then hardened. Teeth have no set, which creates a smooth cut in most materials. Leaving a space between alternate teeth promotes excellent chip removal.
Standard-tooth	Evenly spaced teeth coupled with greater widths makes blades that are hardy and especially suited for gentle curves and straight cuts. May be either pin-end or plain-end.

Standard-Tooth Blades

Standard-tooth blades are still often called simply "scroll saw" blades because for years and years they were the only kind made for a scroll saw. There were no other tooth configurations available.

They are the only blades that some older scrollers will use—and they do a good job for general-purpose scrolling.

Standard-tooth blades have evenly spaced teeth to handle precision inside and outside cuts of irregular shapes. And because standard blades are often wider than other blade types, they handle straight cuts especially well. The added width also makes for a stouter, stiffer blade, which will hold up well under the spring tension that a rigid-arm saw (see page 9) exerts on a blade.

Unlike most of the other tooth configurations, standard blades are available in either 5" or 6" lengths to fit older saws with longer strokes (strokes over $1^1/4$"). Some of the narrower and thinner standard blades can also be used in C-arm, parallel-arm, double-parallel-arm, and oscillating-loop saws.

Standard blades are capable of cutting hard and soft woods, engineered products like plywood and particleboard, and also copper, brass, and aluminum. Teeth per inch (tpi) varies from 7 to 25, with widths up to $1/4$".

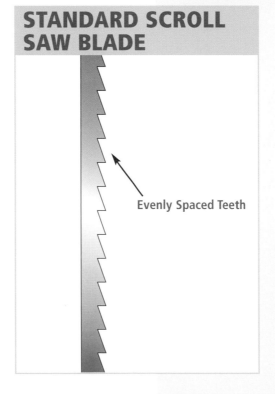

STANDARD SCROLL SAW BLADE

Evenly Spaced Teeth

Skip-Tooth Blades

The first big change in scroll saw blades occurred after parallel-arm and C-arm saws entered the market. Because these saws didn't apply tension to the blades with a heavy-handed spring as the rigid-arm saws did, it was no longer necessary to make the blades wide, stout, and stiff. Because of this, the manufacturing process used to make standard blades

(notching pre-tempered steel to create teeth) quickly changed. Instead of punching, blade makers started milling the blades using soft steel and later heat-treating them to harden the teeth so they'd stay sharp longer.

But what really sets skip-tooth blades apart from their standard-blade predecessors is that the teeth on a skip-tooth blade have no set. That is, alternate teeth are not bent to each side to create clearance for the blade. This meant that the finish left by the blade went from medium-smooth to smooth. What a boon for scrollers everywhere!

As skip-tooth blades evolved, it became evident to manufacturers that if they skipped alternate teeth, the blade was better able to remove sawdust from the kerf and at the same time, keep the blade cooler. The skip-tooth configuration cuts through wood fast, clears dust and chips quickly, and leaves a smooth finish. No wonder it's the most used configuration today. Skip-tooth blades come in sizes ranging from 7 to 33 teeth per inch and can make delicate cuts and tight radii in even the thinnest woods. They can also blow through wood up to 2" in thickness and can produce good results in plastic as well.

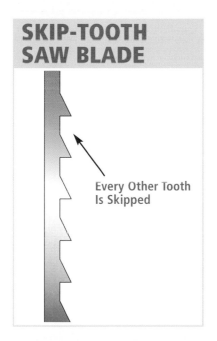

SKIP-TOOTH SAW BLADE

Every Other Tooth Is Skipped

PRECISION-GROUND-TOOTH BLADES

PGT or Precision-Ground-Tooth blades are made exclusively by the Olson Saw Company. What makes these blades unique is that the teeth are ground, rather than milled or notched. The teeth are ground into pre-tempered steel, which creates a tooth with no burr; burrs are common with the other processes. With no burr to affect the cut, PGT blades cut straight and leave a super-smooth finish. PGT blades come in skip- or double-tooth configurations and have reverse teeth at the bottom end of the blade to score the underside of the workpiece. This eliminates tear-out and splintering—something that's essential for projects that will be viewed from all sides.

Reverse-Tooth Blades

Reverse-tooth blades have the same characteristics as skip-tooth blades except that they have reverse teeth on the bottom. The reverse-tooth concept was invented by the Olson Saw Company in Brooklyn, New York, for Playskool. The problem Playskool was having involved their wooden puzzles for children. Bottom tear-out eliminated the bottom layer of a multi-layered wooden puzzle. By using the reverse-tooth blades developed by Olson, Playskool was able to save the bottom layer.

Reverse tooth blades work especially well when cutting plywood—especially premium plywood (page 43)—because they prevent the delicate plies from tearing out. Teeth-per-inch specifications on reverse-tooth blades may seem confusing, as they're typically expressed in two numbers, such as 20/14. The first number indicates how many teeth per inch the blade has; the second number describes how many teeth are reversed at the bottom of the blade. Typical teeth per inch range from 28 to 9½, with the number of reverse teeth varying from 21 to 6 at the end of the blade.

To keep both sides of a workpiece from tearing out, you may have to adjust the blade length or its position in the blade holders so that one to two of the reverse teeth are showing above the saw table on the upstroke of the blade. If you don't adjust the blade for the thickness of the stock you're working with, when scrolling thin materials you may get tear-out on the top of the workpiece.

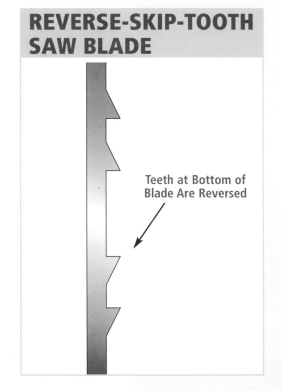

REVERSE-SKIP-TOOTH SAW BLADE

Teeth at Bottom of Blade Are Reversed

Double-Tooth Blades

The double-tooth configuration has a repeating pattern of two teeth together followed by a flat space. This creates efficient chip removal while producing a smooth cut. Double-tooth blades also tend to leave less fuzz on the bottom of a workpiece, and many scrollers feel that these blades offer better control than any other configuration.

Double-tooth blades are available with teeth per inch ranging from 10 up to 33. They work well in both wood and plastic, and in engineered panels like plywood and particleboard. They are not recommended for cutting metal.

For best results, use more teeth per inch for thinner stock and fewer teeth per inch for thicker stock. Also, more teeth per inch produce a finer cut, which works best for softwoods. Fewer teeth per inch create a coarser cut, which does a better job with hardwoods.

Keep in mind that blades with fewer teeth are much stouter than blades with many teeth. So you should always pick a blade with the fewest teeth that can handle both the tightest radii that you'll be turning and the thickness of the stock that you'll be cutting.

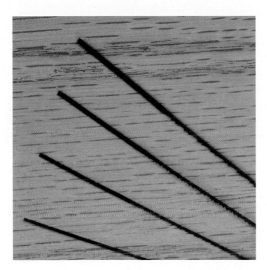

DOUBLE-TOOTH SAW BLADE

Every 3rd Tooth Is Skipped

Crown-Tooth Blades

Crown-tooth blades have milled teeth that cut in both directions. This means that they cut on both the upstroke and downstroke. Crown-tooth blades are another development by the Olson Saw Company. Because the teeth are cutting in opposing directions, cutting action is slowed. This offers better control, which is especially useful when scrolling delicate fretwork.

The finish that these blades produce is very smooth, with clean, splinter-free edges. Crown-tooth blades work well in softwood and hardwoods, and in engineered panels such as plywood and particleboard. What's more, the two-way cutting action prevents melting behind the blade when cutting plastic, which is a real problem with other blades. Crown-tooth blades are recommended for cutting composites such as Corian and SwanStone and plastics like acrylic, Lexan (polycarbonate), fiberglass, and Plexiglas.

Another benefit of these blades is that you can turn the blade upside down for a fresh set of teeth (if you're not cutting thick or stacked material). Additionally, since there is no top or bottom on these blades, installation is a snap. You don't have to hold a blade up to the light and squint at the tiny teeth to figure out which direction they're pointing—since they're pointing both ways, it doesn't matter. Crown-tooth blades come with teeth per inch ranging from 6 to 20.

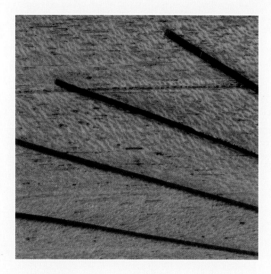

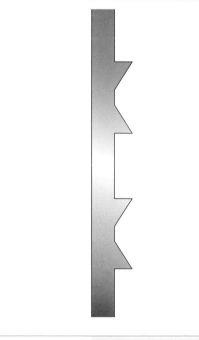

CROWN-TOOTH SAW BLADE

Spiral Blades

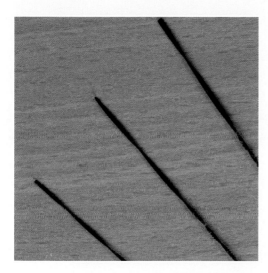

A spiral blade is basically a standard blade that's been twisted to position teeth all the way around the blade. This creates a blade that can cut in all directions and has 360-degree cutting capability. What this means is that you never have to turn the workpiece to make a cut. You don't need to present the workpiece to the blade so the teeth will cut, because the teeth are pointed in all directions.

This actually takes some getting used to: You don't have to turn a workpiece—just push it, pull it, or move it laterally and the blade will cut. Spiral blades are the answer to many difficult sawing challenges. If you've ever watched a scroller effortlessly cut someone's name in a baseball bat without turning the bat once, you've seen a spiral blade in action. Also, crafters who cut names on the slant (for example, for a desk nameplate) can accomplish this only with a spiral blade. With any other blade, you'd have to rotate the workpiece—and therefore orient the blade to the workpiece at a different angle—which would create cone-shaped letters.

Spiral blades come with anywhere from 30 to 51 teeth per inch and are available with twisted ends or flat ends. The last inch or so on flat-end blades are not twisted. This creates a flat end that's easier to install in blade clamps.

Is there any downside to these blades? Yes. Because the teeth are cutting in all directions at all times, they tend to create a rough cut, which is often accompanied by splintering and tear-out of one or both surfaces. So, they're not the ultimate blades, but they are the *only* way to make some cuts.

FLAT-END SPIRAL SAW BLADE

← Blade Is Twisted

Blade Sizes

Once you've decided on a type of scroll saw blade to use, your next decision is about size. Most scroll saw blades use the universal numbering system shown in the chart below to describe how many teeth per inch (tpi) they have.

Teeth-per-inch guidelines

More teeth per inch produce a finer cut, but create a more delicate blade. Fewer teeth per inch provide a rougher cut, but make for a stouter blade. As a general rule, you want to use as few teeth as possible to achieve the desired smoothness you're after. This way, you'll experience less blade breakage. Also, use more teeth with thin stock and fewer teeth for thick stock. With thin stock you want at least two or more teeth in contact with the workpiece to prevent tear-out and blade breakage, as illustrated in the drawing at right.

Most commonly used blades

As you gain experience scrolling, you'll probably find that you reach for the number 5-, 7-, and 9-sized blades the most often (see the top photo). They'll be in either skip-tooth, double-tooth, crown-tooth, or PGT configurations. These stouter blades are perfect for general-purpose work. The number 5 will handle most of the close-radius work you want to do. For cutting plywood, you'll want at least some of these blades to have reverse teeth.

If you plan to delve into fretwork, you'll want to buy some number 2, 3, and 4 blades to handle the tight-radius work involved. Does your interest run to veining work, marquetry, and any work in veneer? Pick up a set of 3/0 and 2/0 number blades to tackle this delicate and intricate work. Finally, it's a good idea to have a couple of spiral blades on hand for those problem cuts that only a spiral blade can tackle.

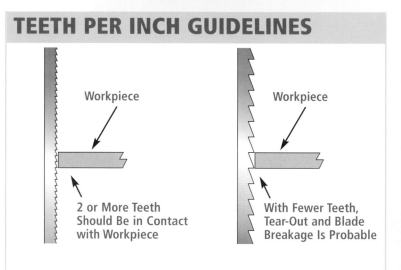

TEETH PER INCH GUIDELINES

Workpiece

2 or More Teeth Should Be in Contact with Workpiece

Workpiece

With Fewer Teeth, Tear-Out and Blade Breakage Is Probable

TYPICAL BLADE SIZES

Universal Number	Teeth Per Inch (Typical)
3/0	33
2/0	28
1	24
2	20
4	15
5	12.5
7	11
9	11
12	9.5

Blade & Table Accessories

Unlike most other power tools, there aren't hundreds of jigs and fixtures made for the scroll saw. The real variety of product available is in blades (pages 28–36). There are, however, quite a few accessories that can make your scrolling easier and more enjoyable.

Stands

One of the accessories that many scrollers purchase is a stand for their saw. Saw stands keep bench-top saws from taking up bench space and raise the saw to the proper working height. The quality of stands varies tremendously, from stamped-steel stands that are bolted together like an Erector set (rear stand in top photo) to heavy-duty metal tubing and braces welded together (front stand in top photo). Naturally, a stand that's welded together is going to hold up better over time, while also virtually eliminating vibration. Make sure the stand you buy has built-in levelers to level the stand on your shop floor. Alternatively, you can build your own stand; see pages 123–128 for plans for a stand with storage.

Arm lifts

Scrollers who do a lot of fretwork find an arm lift invaluable. Arm lifts are usually foot-activated mechanisms that lift the upper arm high above the saw table, as shown in the middle photo. The extra space created between the upper arm and the saw table provides better access when threading blades up through holes to make pierced cuts. Arm lifts come standard on some saws, but may also be purchased as an add-on accessory.

QUICK-RELEASE BLADE KITS

If you own an older scroll saw that has conventional screw-type blade clamps, do yourself a favor and buy a quick-release blade kit. Upgrade kits are available from specific saw manufacturers or for generic use on any saw, as shown in the bottom photo. The wasted time and frustration of fighting screw-type clamps will fade away as soon as you install a set of these quick-release clamps. Whenever possible, replace both the top and bottom clamp pads; if you can do only one, do the top pad.

Add-on dust blowers

Many older scroll saws do not have built-in blowers to keep the kerf being cut on a workpiece free from dust. On those that do, the tubing that runs between the diaphragm and the directional nozzle is often kinked or damaged. You can find an add-on dust blower kit in most mail-order woodworking catalogs. These consist of plastic tubing, an articulated arm, and a set of cable clamps for attaching the tubing. You can use this to replace a defective line and upgrade to a better nozzle, or to install a blower on a saw that didn't have one. Air pressure is provided by an off-the-shelf aquarium pump. For more on installing an add-on dust blower, see page 153.

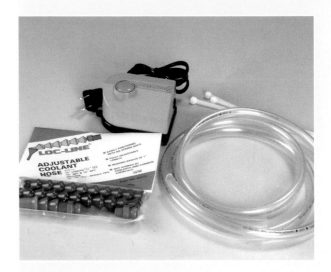

Foot pedals

Most serious scrolling enthusiasts use a foot pedal to turn their saw on and off (middle photo). The saw plugs into the back of the pedal, and the pedal plug is inserted in a wall outlet. The pedal serves as a simple make-or-break connection to control power to the saw. It's a whole lot easier to step on a pedal than it is to reach over and toggle a power switch on and off. This is particularly true for saws that have awkwardly placed power switches. Foot pedals can be bought through most mail-order woodworking catalogs and wherever scrolling supplies are sold.

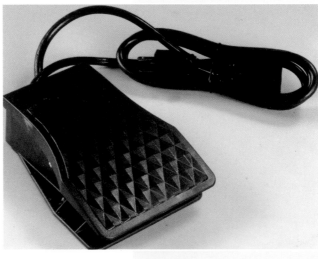

Flexible shafts

Another excellent accessory that's saw-specific is a flexible shaft like the one shown in the bottom photo. One end of the shaft attaches to a hub on the side of the saw; the other end has a collet to accept different bits. Drill bits, files, and sanding disks can all be used here. Fitted with a drill bit, the flexible arm can be used to drill access holes for pierced work. What's really nice is that you don't even have to get up to drill one—just grab the flexible shaft and drill. This is really handy when you find you've inadvertently missed drilling a hole.

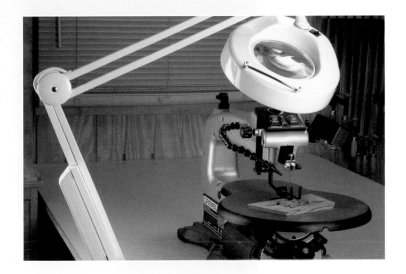

Magnifiers and lights

Scrollers young and old will benefit from mounting a light near their saw to better illuminate their work. An even better choice than a light alone is a light/magnifier combination like the one shown in the top photo. The magnifier is especially useful for working on delicate fretwork. Lights like these can be found at most home centers and hardware stores. Hobby and craft stores often carry them for folks who work with miniatures.

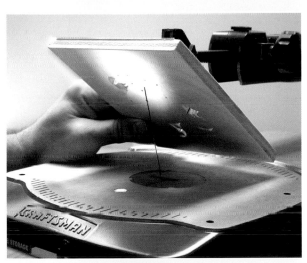

Up lighting

FretLite is a recent innovation by the Olson Saw Company that makes threading blades through workpieces much easier. FretLite is a small light that mounts to the underside of your saw table. It shines a narrowly focused beam of light up through a hole that you drill in your top to illuminate the underside of the workpiece, as shown in the middle photo. This is hugely useful when you're dealing with narrow blades and tiny access holes, such as when scrolling delicate fretwork or marquetry and anytime you're cutting veneer.

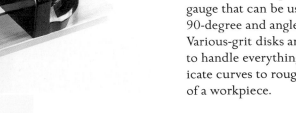

Sanding attachments

Another accessory that's saw-specific is a sanding disk and table that attaches to the side of the saw, as shown in the bottom photo. Since much of the scrollwork that you may do involves curves, it makes a lot of sense to have a sanding disk nearby. The small table is slotted to accept a miter gauge that can be used to sand 90-degree and angled cuts. Various-grit disks are available to handle everything from delicate curves to rough shaping of a workpiece.

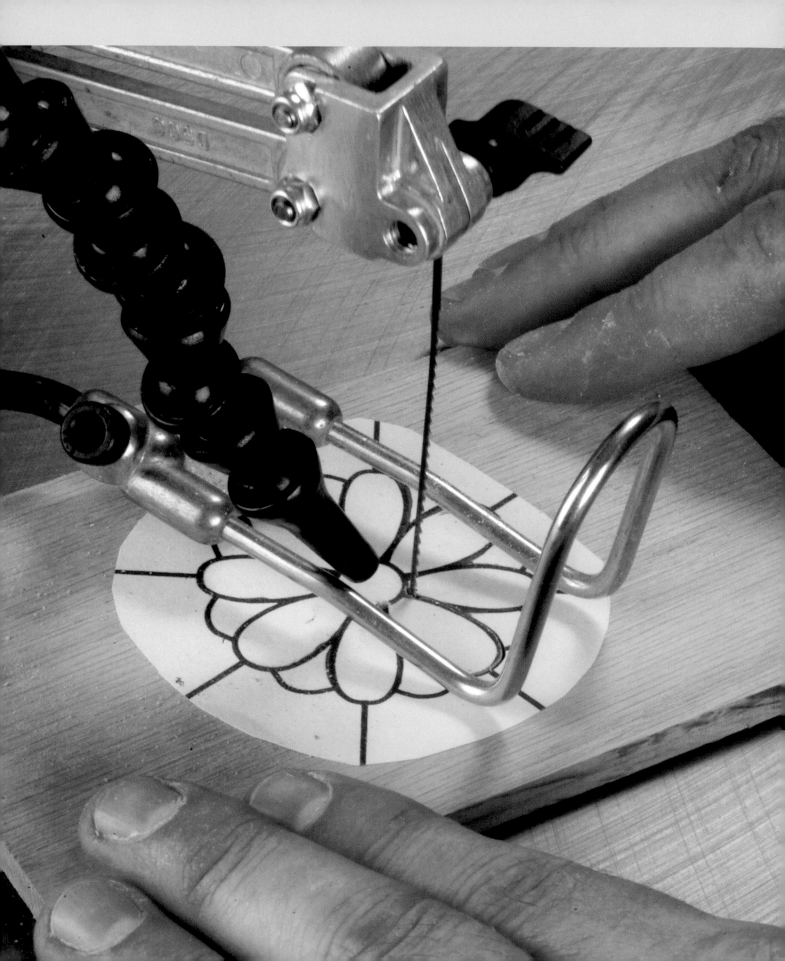

3 Basic Scroll Saw Techniques

There are very few stationary power tools that most woodworkers consider to be "plug and play." The drill press is one—the scroll saw is another. Once you learn how to choose and install blades, you can start scrolling. Sure, there are plenty of techniques to learn such as making straight and curved cuts, on-the-spot corners and turns, as well as nifty tricks like power sanding on the scroll saw. But the scroll saw really is a fairly intuitive and easy-to-use machine.

What may take some learning is preparing a workpiece for scrolling: This can include everything from what material to use to ways to reduce and enlarge a pattern, as well as techniques for affixing a pattern to a workpiece. This chapter will cover all of this and more, along with ways to work safer and smarter.

The small blade of a scroll saw allows you to make cuts that you can't with any other power tool. Even seemingly impossible cuts like the on-the-spot turn shown in the photo on the opposite page can be made with little effort.

Materials for Scrolling

When most folks think about scroll-sawing, they think about wood parts with intricate fretwork. That's because solid wood is the most commonly sawn material. But a well-adjusted saw can cut a variety of materials in addition to solid wood, including plastic, composites, metal, and plywood.

Solid wood

Most scroll saws can tackle solid wood ranging from paper-thin veneer up to 1" or thicker stock (top photo). Many scroll saw projects call for wood that's less than $3/4$" thick. Common thicknesses are $1/8$", $1/4$", $3/8$", and $1/2$". You can buy thin stock from many mail-order woodworking catalogs. Just be aware that thin stock can be quite expensive, and it's sold by the square foot (not by the board foot), or in precut lengths and widths. If you have a well-equipped shop, you can make your own thin stock; see pages 44–45 for more on this.

Plastic

Plastic (middle photo) can be cut easily on most scroll saws, using either a precision-ground-tooth or crown-tooth blade (see pages 31 and 34, respectively). Plastics that cut well include acrylic and sheet plastic, such as Plexiglas. For tips and techniques on working with plastic, see page 72.

Composites

Composites, like those shown in the bottom photo, are primarily used for outdoor building, including but not limited to decks, patios, and outdoor furniture. Composites are typically a hybrid of plastic mixed with wood chips. Because the chips are small and coated with plastic, the material tends to be very stable—and virtually impervious to weather. Common brands include TREX, ChoiceDek, and TimberTech. Composites can be found at most large home centers and some lumberyards.

Metal

Nonferrous metal like thin aluminum (top photo) can be safely cut on the scroll saw with special metal-cutting blades that have more teeth per inch, so they can saw through thin metal. These special blades tend to be stouter—both wider and thicker—than conventional blades. For more on working with metal, see page 73.

Plywood

Because plywood is made up of layers of veneer glued together with the grain running perpendicular on alternate plies, it's very strong and dimensionally stable. The difference between hardwood and softwood plywood has to do with the outer or face veneers. On hardwood plywood, the face veneers are hardwood; on softwood plywood, they are softwood. Both use softwood for the inner plies. Hardwood plywood is the best choice for scrolling, as the face veneers are smoother and more appealing than softwood plywood (middle photo). Most home centers and lumberyards stock some hardwood plywood: typically red oak and birch in $1/4$" and $3/4$" thicknesses.

PREMIUM PLYWOOD

If you're planning on scroll-sawing plywood for a project, consider buying premium plywood (bottom photo). These high-grade plywoods differ from conventional plywood in that there are more, thinner plies sandwiched between the outer veneers. For example, a piece of $3/4$"-thick premium plywood has 13 plies total, compared to 7 in standard plywood. This does a couple of things. First, more plies means greater stability and a much higher strength-to-weight ratio. Second, unlike the unattractive edges of standard plywood, premium plywood offers a unique, attractive edge that can be cleanly machined.

Making Thin Stock

Many of the projects you'll make on the scroll saw will call for thin stock. You can purchase thin stock, but it's expensive. Basically, you're paying for the labor required to saw, plane, or sand down thicker stock. A more economical approach is to make your own thin stock. Depending on what tools you have, you can resaw thicker stock on the table saw or band saw, or plane it with a portable power planer.

Thin stock on the table saw

A simple way to make thin stock is to resaw a board on the table saw into two thinner pieces. Whenever the workpiece you're resawing is wider than the maximum cut on your saw, you'll need to make the cut in two passes. In most cases, it's best to resaw in two equal passes—that is, adjust the blade height to cut one-half the width of the workpiece. Also, it's always wise to use a featherboard when resawing. This will help keep the workpiece pressed firmly against the rip fence as you cut, and also help keep the workpiece from tilting. Raise the blade to the desired cut, turn on the saw, and make your first pass (top photo). Then flip the workpiece end-for-end, taking care to keep the same face pressed up against the rip fence, and make the second pass. There are two options here. One is to have the blade high enough to completely cut the piece in half. If you're using a zero-clearance insert (see the sidebar at right), this works just fine. The only challenge is to guide the thin piece between the saw blade and rip fence safely past the blade. The other option is

to lower the blade so you don't cut all the way through—just very close. Then you can separate the two pieces and hand-plane away the remnants of the thin connecting piece.

ZERO-CLEARANCE INSERT

The opening in most saw throat plates ranges from 3/8" to 5/8". As a workpiece on edge passes over this opening, there's little to support the stock. When you finish cutting through the workpiece, the piece against the rip fence can fall into this opening, possibly jamming against the blade. To prevent this and to provide maximum bearing surface for the workpiece, use a zero-clearance insert when resawing (see the drawing at right).

INSERT WITH BUILT-IN SPLITTER

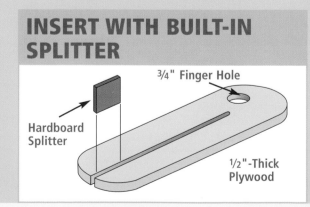

3/4" Finger Hole

Hardboard Splitter

1/2"-Thick Plywood

Thin stock on the band saw

Resawing on the band saw is a technique where you cut through the width of the workpiece to create thinner stock. To resaw on a band saw, you'll need to support the wood during the cut (since it's on its edge), with a fence like the one shown in the top photo. Install a resaw blade (these have fewer teeth per inch than standard band saw blades) and increase the blade tension to at least the next blade width. Then lower the blade guard as close to the workpiece as possible and clamp the fence to the table for the desired cut. Turn on the saw and guide the workpiece into the blade. Use steady, even pressure. As you complete the cut, use a push block to safely push the workpiece past the saw blade.

PLANING THIN STOCK

Although most manufacturers have built-in stops on their power planers that limit how close the cutterhead can come to the planer's bed, woodworkers commonly get around this by using an auxiliary platform that lets the cutterhead be closer to the workpiece. Be warned that thin wood can shatter in the planer with this method. If you choose to make your own thin stock this way, make sure you don't stand directly behind or in front of the planer. Wear safety glasses, take thin cuts, and make sure that the planer's knives are sharp.

There are two common ways to plane thin stock on a power planer: with a sled that hooks onto the planer's bed, and with a sled that you feed through the planer. The advantage of a hook-on sled is that you can plane multiple pieces easily. A hook-on sled has a cleat on the front edge that hooks onto the bed of the planer, see the drawing at right. The stock slides on the sled through the planer.

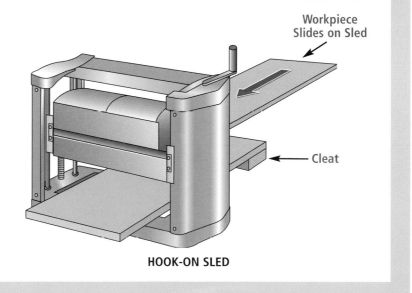

Workpiece Slides on Sled

Cleat

HOOK-ON SLED

Working with Patterns

Most cutting on a scroll saw is done following a pattern. Patterns may be either full or half and can be traced or attached to the workpiece.

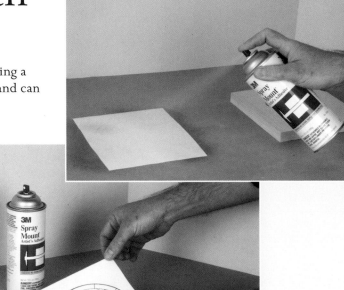

Full patterns

For intricate full patterns like the one shown at right, most scrollers prefer to attach the pattern directly to the workpiece with some type of adhesive. Typically a spray-on adhesive is applied to the back of the pattern, and then it's pressed in place on the workpiece (top two photos). Alternatively, if the pattern is simple, you can cut it out, hold it in place on the workpiece, and trace around it with a pencil.

Half patterns

Half patterns are commonly used to save space in a project book or article when both sides of the pattern are identical. To transfer this type of pattern to a workpiece, start by drawing a centerline directly on the workpiece as shown in the photo at right. Then position the pattern so its centerline aligns with the centerline you just marked on the workpiece. Trace around the pattern with a pencil. Next, flip the pattern over, realign the centerline, and trace around the edges as shown in the bottom photo.

Unless the project you're scrolling has moving or separate parts, the pattern will have small wooden bridges called ties that connect all the elements of the design together. If you want to make your own pattern, or adopt a drawing or photo to make it into a pattern, you'll have to incorporate ties to bridge together isolated parts of the pattern.

Ties

Take the drawing in the top photo, for example. If you wanted to cut out the silhouette tractor, the front and rear wheel would be separate pieces as drawn. Here's where you'd need to add ties as shown to connect the tires to the body of the tractor.

Likewise, you couldn't cut out the wheels as shown because the axles would be separate pieces. To get around this, draw a set of ties to resemble spokes on a tire as shown in the middle photo. This way, you can cut out the spaces between the spokes, and the spokes will connect the tires to the axles.

Line continuity

Often overlooked as a source of patterns for scroll sawing are the patterns used to make stained glass. These work particularly well for intarsia and marquetry projects; see pages 98 and 107, respectively. If you decide to use a stained glass pattern for standard scroll sawing, you'll need to continue some of the pattern lines to form ties to hold the design together (bottom photo). That's because stained glass parts are soldered together to create a single unit—not something that will work with standard scrolling. Also, you may want to eliminate some of the parts to simplify the design, as shown in the leaf portion of the pattern shown in the bottom photo.

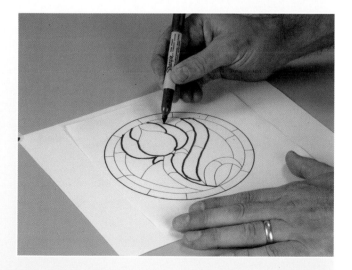

Enlarging & Reducing Patterns

Often the pattern you want to use will be either too big or too small. There are many ways to enlarge or reduce patterns. The easiest is to use a copy machine that can reduce or enlarge—you'll find one at most office-supply stores. If you'd rather use your time in the shop instead of traveling to a store, consider one of the two methods described here: using graph paper or using a pantograph.

Using graph paper

You can reduce or enlarge a pattern using graph paper and a little patience. In the example shown in the top two photos, we're doubling the size of the original pattern. To do this, start by taping the original pattern to a piece of graph paper. Then define the limits of the new pattern by marking dots on the blank paper to indicate the widest and longest points of the pattern, as shown in the top photo. For straight lines, connect the dots using a straightedge and a pencil.

Next, use the original pattern to identify points along any curved portions of the perimeter. Mark these on the new pattern in the correspondingly larger or smaller locations. Then all that's left is to connect the dots. You can draw curved parts freehand (as shown in the middle photo), or use a flexible curve or a French curve; see page 54 for more on these common drafting tools.

Using a pantograph

A pantograph is a special drawing aid that loosely resembles an accordion-style clothes rack; it lets you easily enlarge or reduce patterns. You can buy these or make your own; see pages 133–138 for detailed instructions on how to build a pantograph. A pantograph has a pair of styluses: One has a metal tip that you

use to trace the original pattern, and the second stylus holds a pencil. This pencil traces a smaller or larger pattern on a blank piece of paper as you trace over the original pattern with the metal stylus. To use a pantograph, start by clamping the fixed pivot point to the edge of a table or drawing board, as shown in the bottom photo.

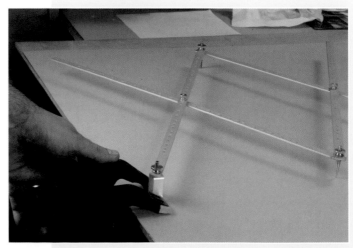

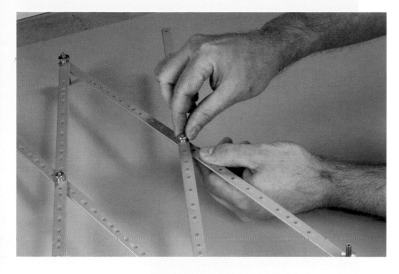

Once the fixed pivot point is secured, adjust the pantograph to the desired reduction or enlargement by moving the legs of the pantograph. The legs are held together with removable nuts and bolts that pass through a series of holes drilled in each leg; marks on the legs describe the amount of reduction/enlargement usually in terms of a ratio. For example, if you wanted to double the size of a pattern, you'd connect the legs together at the 2:1 hole locations as shown in the top photo.

With the pantograph set up, the next step is to position the original pattern and a blank sheet

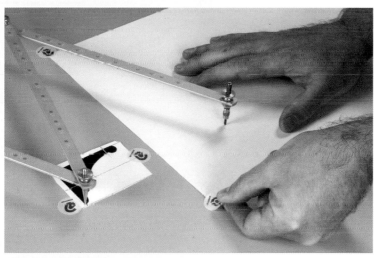

of paper for the new pattern. Place the original pattern close to the fixed pivot point and secure it to the work surface (we used drafting dots for this, as they're convenient and easy to remove, but masking tape works just as well). Then place the metal stylus on the far left edge of the original pattern. Position the blank sheet so the pencil stylus is near the left edge of the blank sheet, as shown in the middle photo. Once everything is in place, secure the blank sheet to the work surface.

To enlarge or reduce the pattern, simply trace the original pattern with the metal stylus; the pencil stylus will trace the new pattern on the blank sheet of paper as shown in the bottom photo. Move the metal stylus slowly, and take care to lift the pencil stylus if you need to move the metal stylus location to trace another section. If you don't lift it and just move the metal stylus, the pencil will draw this movement on the new pattern.

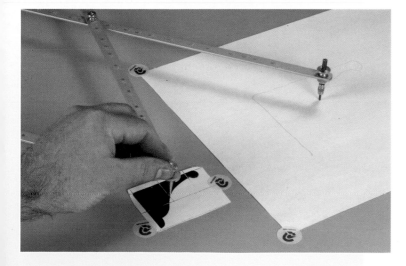

Freehand Tracing

In addition to enlarging and reducing patterns, you'll often need to simply duplicate a pattern. Here again, a copy machine makes this easy. But most folks don't have one of these in the home. In lieu of a copy machine, you can copy a pattern freehand with either tracing paper or carbon paper.

Carbon paper

With the advent of computers and printers capable of spewing out multiple copies of a document, good old-fashioned carbon paper is getting harder to find these days. It still works great, though. Just slip a piece of it between the pattern and the workpiece (or the pattern and a blank sheet of paper, as shown in the top photo), and trace the pattern. A ballpoint pen works best for tracing—especially the roller-ball type—because it slides effortlessly across the pattern with little risk of tearing.

Tracing paper

Tracing paper is also an excellent material to use for duplicating patterns. This tissue-thin material does have a tendency to tear easily, so it's best to use a felt-tip marker to reduce the risk of damage. Lay a piece over the pattern, and secure the edges with masking tape or drafting dots to prevent it from sliding around as you trace (middle photo).

Hand position

Freehand tracing does require some rudimentary drawing skills and a bit of patience. One way to help create smooth lines is to rest the heel of your hand on the drawing surface as you trace, as shown in the bottom photo. This creates a solid foundation and virtually eliminates any shakiness that's common when the tracing hand is unsupported. Whenever possible, try to draw continuous lines; any starts or stops will likely add bumps in the pattern lines.

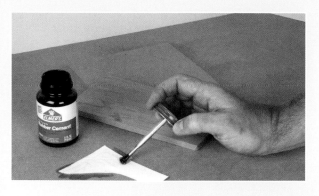

Bonding Patterns

If you're planning to use a paper pattern, you'll need to decide on an adhesive for attaching the pattern to the workpiece. The two most commonly used adhesives are rubber cement and spray-on adhesive.

Rubber cement

In the past, scrollers relied on rubber cement to fasten paper patterns to wood (top photo). It works well but is losing out to spray-on adhesives, which many find more convenient. Rubber cement comes with a built-in applicator attached to the screw-on lid. Brush on a light coat and allow it to dry for about 15 seconds. Then position it over the workpiece and press it in place. If needed, the cement will let you rotate and shift the pattern for a bit before it sets up.

Spray-on adhesive

There are a few of advantages to spraying on adhesive (middle photo): It goes on fast, the coating typically is uniform and even (as long as you don't pause in one spot as you spray), and the adhesive holds well. It's important to spray on a light coat, or else you could end up spending time trying to scrape the paper off the wood once you're done scrolling. It's also a good idea to clear the nozzle after each use to prevent it from clogging; just hold the can upside down and press the nozzle down until just air comes out, as shown in the inset photo.

DOUBLE-SIDED TIP FOR THIN STOCK

If the wood you're cutting is extremely thin or fragile, try this handy trick to help support the wood fibers. Once you've attached the pattern on the top of the workpiece, attach a blank piece of paper to the bottom (bottom photo). This works really well on projects calling for stock ¼" and thinner, where you'll be cutting intricate patterns, such as those for Christmas ornaments.

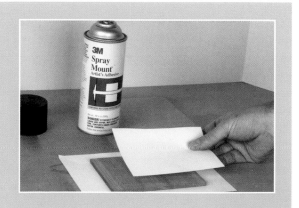

Transfer Tools

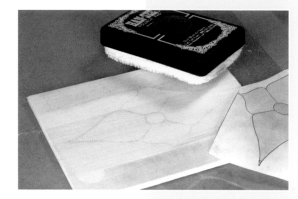

Another method of transferring patterns called pouncing has been used for years by sign-makers and sewing professionals. Here, a barbed wheel called a pouncing wheel is traced around the pattern. This creates tiny holes in the pattern that, when placed over a workpiece and "pounced" with colored dust, leaves a dotted duplicate of the pattern, as shown in the top photo.

Pouncing wheel

Pouncing tools are sold at most sign-supply stores and have very sharp teeth. You can also find a version of this where sewing supplies are sold; it's usually called a pattern wheel or dart wheel, but the barb tips are not anywhere near as sharp as a traditional pouncing tool. To transfer a pattern, attach the original pattern to a piece of cardboard. Then, trace the pattern with the pouncing wheel as shown in the second photo.

When you've traced the entire pattern, remove it from the cardboard and flip the pattern over. You should see tiny ridges where the pouncing wheel did its work. These need to be removed with a sanding block (as shown in the photo at right) to create the tiny holes for the dust to pass through.

Now you can attach the pattern to your workpiece and use a pouncing stick or pad (like the one shown in the bottom photo) to pounce the pattern. You can order pouncing dust in black or white (for pouncing on dark woods) or make your own by sanding a pencil lead, artist's charcoal sticks, or colored chalk. Make your own pouncing pad by wrapping light fabric around a ball of cotton infused with the dust you made. Then simply pounce it on the pattern. Remove the pattern carefully and save any excess dust. Both the pouncing dust and the pattern can be used over and over.

Transferring patterns with heat

If the patterns you're using for a project were made on a copy machine, there's one other technique you can use to transfer the pattern to the workpiece: heat. Because the toner used to make the pattern copy is heat-sensitive, you can reheat it and it will melt and fuse to the workpiece. For years, woodworkers have used a standard household iron for this (see the sidebar below), but now there are specialty transfer tools available for this like the one shown in the top photo.

A transfer tool looks like a small soldering iron but instead of a pointed tip, it has a flat, smooth tip about the size of a quarter. After allowing the tool to heat up the recommended time, you simply place the pattern on the workpiece with the printed side down and press the transfer tool against the pattern, as shown in the middle photo. The type of wood and the darkness of the copy will determine how fast or slow you need to move the transfer tool. As a general rule, if you see the paper discolor slightly, the pattern has been successfully transferred. One advantage of a transfer tool over a household iron? The smaller head lets you follow the pattern lines and ensures that a clean, crisp pattern is transferred.

TRANSFERRING PATTERNS WITH AN IRON

You don't need a special transfer tool (like the one described above) to transfer a copied pattern onto a workpiece—an ordinary iron will also do the job. Set the iron for cotton and make sure not to use steam. When heated, "iron" the pattern onto the workpiece, taking care to keep the iron constantly moving to prevent scorching the wood. Tip: When you're done with the iron, make sure to clean it up before returning it to the rightful owner—that is, if you ever want to borrow it again.

Working with Templates

For projects that call for multiples of the same part, you may find it worthwhile to make a template. A template allows you to better fit parts on stock (see the drawing on the opposite page). And because you trace around them with a pencil, there's no paper to remove or mess to clean up.

Template stock

Because it has no grain and is so dimensionally stable, hardboard (either ⅛"-thick or ¼"-thick) is perfect for making templates. You can make a template by either drawing freehand on the hardboard, or attaching a pattern (as shown in the photo below) directly to the hardboard and cutting it to shape. The edges sand well and remain crisp over time, resulting in an accurate pattern that can be used for years.

BASIC DRAFTING TOOLS

Over time, most woodworkers develop some basic drawing skills, since they often have to sketch out a thought, pattern, or construction detail for a project. There are a number of basic drafting tools that can make this easier and more accurate. A basic kit is comprised of these tools:

Mechanical or drafting pencil. Replaceable leads of uniform diameter make this the best tool for drawing lines of consistent width.

Rule. A plastic rule is light and comfortable to work with and can't damage the drawing paper, as metal or wood rules can; graduations should be in inches and centimeters. It's a good idea to have both a 12" and an 18" rule on hand for larger drawing projects.

Triangle. The 30-60-90-degree triangle shown in the inset photo is the best all-purpose triangle you can buy; these are the angles commonly used to draw an isometric drawing.

Circle template. It's easy to draw perfect circles with a circle template; the crosshairs on the punched holes let you accurately draw aligned circles.

Compass. A compass is handy for circles larger than what the circle template can handle, and it's also useful for drawing arcs.

Protractor. One of the simplest ways to find and draw an angle is to use a protractor.

Flexible curve. A flexible curve allows you to draw smooth, flowing curves of almost any size and shape; just bend the curve to the shape you want and trace around it.

If in doubt, make a template
Not sure whether you'll be making multiples of the project you're working on? With no extra work, you can make a template by simply inserting a piece of thin hardboard between pattern and stock before you cut out the shape, as shown in the top photo. Just make sure to secure the hardboard to the workpiece with rubber cement or spray-on adhesive to keep it from sliding about as you cut out the shape. When done, you'll have your project piece—and a pattern to reuse in the future.

GROUPING PATTERNS TO CONSERVE STOCK

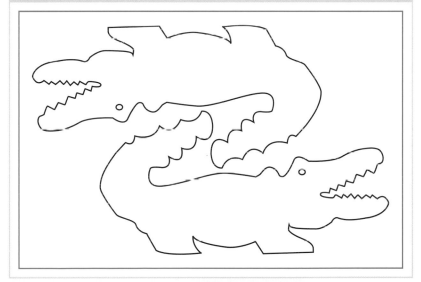

Grouping patterns
One technique that can save you money when working with templates is to group your patterns to conserve stock. If grain direction isn't an issue, you can rotate and flop templates as needed to get them close together; see the middle drawing. This is something that's just not easily done when you use a paper pattern, unless you go to the trouble of cutting out the pattern.

Plastic templates show grain
A final tip for working with templates: Instead of using hardboard to make a template, use thin plastic. A thin plastic template, like the one shown in the bottom photo, lets the grain show through so you can move the template around to get the best color and grain pattern. (For more on working with plastic, see page 72.)

Starting points

Every project part that you scroll-cut will have one or more sets of starting and stopping points. These are not identified on the pattern. It's up to you to decide the locations. Experienced scrollers know that there are good places and bad places to start and stop cuts.

Start and stop points

If you're a beginning scroller, give starting and stopping points some thought before beginning work on a part. It's a good idea to actually mark points on the pattern where you intend to drill holes if needed for pierced cuts, as shown in the top photo. Imagine yourself making the cut. Follow the path of the saw blade and try to identify any areas where you might run into problems. Experience will teach you the best places for starting points—and places to avoid.

Access hole guidelines

There are no hard and fast rules for placing access holes in a project, but there are some general guidelines that will make scrolling easier and more enjoyable if you follow them. First, whenever a design calls for a very sharp turn, consider drilling an access hole at the curve with a drill bit that matches the diameter of the curve. Second, when two lines intersect to form a point, an access hole right at the tip of the point will let you go in either direction, as shown in the middle drawing. Third, access holes are free—mark and drill as many as you like in order to make cutting the pattern as easy as possible.

Access placement to avoid

If you place an access hole directly on or close to a gradual curve (as shown in the bottom photo), odds are you'll find it very difficult to scroll a smooth curve. That's because you'll be starting and stopping on the curve itself—and this usually leads to a bump in the curve, which will later have to be sanded off. Avoid this by placing the access holes at the beginning or end of the curve so you can cut the curve in one smooth pass.

ACCESS HOLE LOCATIONS

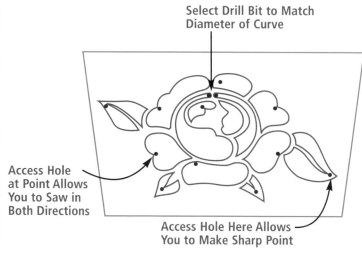

Select Drill Bit to Match Diameter of Curve

Access Hole at Point Allows You to Saw in Both Directions

Access Hole Here Allows You to Make Sharp Point

Note: Red dots are suggested positions for access holes.

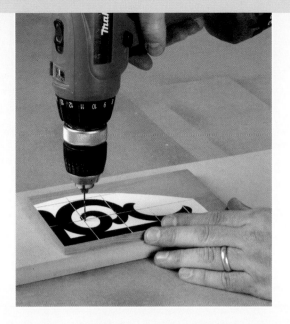

Drilling access holes

Once your access holes are marked on the pattern, you can drill them with a portable drill (as shown in the top photo) or on the drill press. In either case, make sure to slip a backer board underneath the workpiece to back up the drill bit as it exits the workpiece; this will leave a clean, crisp hole. (A backer board will also protect your work surface or drill press table.) Because a drill press provides accurate vertical drilling, it's a better choice than a portable drill, which can easily drill an access hole at an angle if not held perfectly perpendicular to the workpiece. An angled hole makes it harder to thread a blade though the workpiece for a pierced cut.

Removing exit-side tear-out

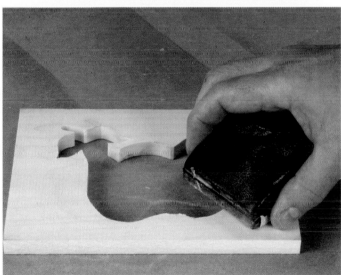

To get an accurate cut on the scroll saw, the workpiece must lie flat on the table. Drilling often causes tear-out on the bottom of the workpiece, which can cause it to rest on the table at an angle. After you've drilled your access holes, it's smart to flip the workpiece over and knock off any protruding wood fibers with a sanding block. This same technique is useful as you scroll. Unless you're using a reverse-tooth blade (see page 32), odds are that cutting will produce tear-out. So occasionally stop scrolling, flip the piece over, and flatten the back with a sanding block (middle photo).

Pierced cut holes

Whenever you need to drill an access hole for a pierced cut, it's important to know which type of blade you'll be using (pin-end or plain-end) and the size. Pin-end blades generally need much larger access holes in order for the pinned end to fit through the hole. Blade widths vary tremendously as well, and in many cases a large hole isn't possible, as it would be unsightly. The general idea is to make the hole just large enough for the blade to pass through with a little extra for clearance, as shown in the bottom photo. Just remember that the smaller the hole diameter, the more challenging it is to thread the blade.

Selecting the Right Blade

Selecting the blade for a project can mean the difference between smooth, easy scrolling and blade breakage and frustration. For more on blade types, see pages 29–36. Once you've chosen a type, you'll need to select the correct size. Blades are sized by their number of teeth per inch; see the chart below.

Generally, more teeth per inch provide a finer cut, which works well in softwoods. Fewer teeth per inch provide a coarser cut, which is good for hardwoods. Use the highest-number blade possible since larger blades are more durable. Also, select low-number blades for tight radii and high-number blades for more general-purpose work. You'll also find that lower-number blades work better for thinner stock and higher numbers for thicker stock.

BLADE SELECTION CHART

Tooth Style	Univ. No.	TPI*	Width	Thickness	Access Hole	Application	Finish
Skip	3/0	33	.022"	.008"	1/32"	Super-intricate sawing in thin wood and veneer	Smooth
Skip	2/0	28	.022"	.010"	1/32"	Intricate sawing in thin softwoods and veneer	Smooth
Skip	2	20	.029"	.012"	3/64"	Tight-radius work in softwoods up to 3/4"	Smooth
Skip	4	15	.035"	.015"	1/16"	Tight-radius work in softwoods and plywood up to 3/4"	Smooth
Skip	5	12.5	.038"	.016"	1/16"	Close-radius cutting of thin hard- and softwoods up to 3/4"	Smooth
Skip	7	11.5	.045"	.017"	1/16"	General-purpose cutting of soft- and hardwoods up to 3/4" thick	Smooth
Skip	9	11.5	.053"	.018"	1/16"	General-purpose cutting of hard- and softwoods, and plywood	Smooth
Skip	12	9.5	.062"	.024"	5/64"	Heavy-duty for fast cuts in hard- and softwoods, and plywood	Smooth
Double	3/0	33	.023"	.008"	1/32"	Super-intricate sawing in veneer and thin softwood	Smooth
Double	2/0	37	.023"	.011"	1/32"	Marquetry in thin wood and veneer	Smooth
Double	1	30	.026"	.013"	3/64"	Delicate fretwork in softwoods up to 3/4" thick	Smooth
Double	3	23	.032"	.014"	3/64"	Intricate sawing of softwoods up to 1 1/2" thick	Smooth
Double	5	16	.038"	.016"	1/16"	Tight-radius work in softwoods up to 1 1/2" thick	Smooth
Double	7	13	.044"	.018"	1/16"	Close-radius cutting in soft- and hardwoods up to 3/4" thick	Smooth
Double	9	11	.053"	.018"	1/16"	General-purpose cutting of soft- and hardwoods up to 1 1/2" thick	Smooth
Double	12	10	.061"	.022"	5/64"	Heavy-duty cuts in stock up to 1 1/2" and plywood	Smooth
Metal	n/a	30	.041"	.019"	n/a	Very thin metal sheets	Medium
Metal	n/a	25	.049"	.022"	n/a	Thin metal sheets	Medium
Metal	n/a	20	.070"	.023"	n/a	Thicker metal sheets	Medium
Reverse	2/0	28/21*	.022"	.010"	1/32"	Extreme-radius cutting in thin softwood/veneer	Splinter-free
Reverse	2R	20/14*	.029"	.012"	3/64"	Delicate fretwork in softwoods up to 3/4" thick	Splinter-free
Reverse	5R	12/9*	.038"	.016"	3/64"	Close-radius work in softwoods up to 1 1/2" thick	Splinter-free
Reverse	7R	11/8*	.047"	.017"	1/16"	General-purpose work in soft- and hardwoods up to 3/4" thick	Splinter-free
Reverse	9R	11/8*	.054"	.019"	1/16"	General-purpose work in soft- and hardwoods up to 1 1/2" & plywood	Splinter-free
Reverse	12R	9.5/6*	.062"	.024"	5/64"	Heavy-duty for fast cuts in soft- and hardwoods up to 1 1/2" & plywood	Splinter-free
Spiral	0	n/a	n/a	.032"	3/64"	Bevel-cut letters and workpieces too large to turn, up to 3/4" thick	Rough
Spiral	2	n/a	n/a	.035"	5/64"	Bevel-cut letters and workpieces too large to turn, up to 1 1/2" thick	Rough
Spiral	4	n/a	n/a	.041"	7/64"	Bevel-cut letters and workpieces too large to turn, up to 1 1/2" thick	Rough

*teeth per inch and number of reverse teeth (if applicable)

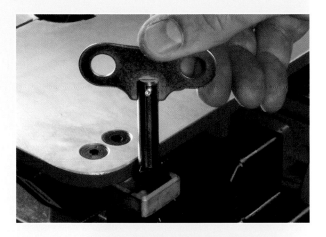

Preparing to Cut

Okay, you have your pattern attached to your workpiece, access holes are drilled, and you've selected a blade. You're not quite ready to scroll—not until you've installed the blade, tensioned it properly, and checked the table. How you change blades and tension them will depend on your saw. There are two basic methods used to hold blades in place: clamp pads that are engaged by tightening a screw, and clamp pads that engage via a quick-release mechanism.

Changing screw type blades

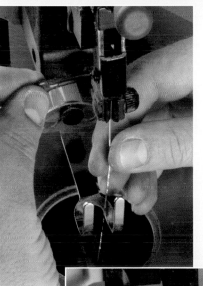

To change the blade on a screw-type clamp mechanism, first remove the entire blade assembly from the saw after the tension has been released. Saws like the Hegner shown in the top photo have a special blade clamp holder attached to the side of the saw table. Insert one of the blade clamps in the holder and use the wrench provided to loosen the screw. Remove the old blade, insert the desired one with the teeth facing forward and down, and tighten the screw; repeat for the other end. Then reinstall the blade assembly and tension the blade.

Quick-release clamps

Scroll saws with quick-release clamp pads make changing blades a snap. Start by removing the table insert, and release the blade tension. Then push the upper blade-locking lever to release the blade, as shown in the middle photo. This should release the blade from the upper clamp pads. Next, push the locking lever on the lower clamp pad to the rear, as shown in the bottom photo. This will release the blade, allowing you to remove it. To install a new blade, insert it in the upper clamp pads with the teeth forward and facing down and pull the locking lever forward to secure the blade; repeat for the bottom. Then tension the blade and reinstall the table insert.

Tension controls

There are about as many different blade-tensioning setups as there are different scroll saws. Consult your owner's manual for the recommended tensioning procedure. Tension controls are typically located at either the rear of the saw (as shown in the top photo) or in the front of the saw on the top of the arm. Rear tensioning controls like the one shown here are usually adjusted by releasing the cam lock, rotating the lever, and then re-engaging the cam lock. A front tension control is more convenient to use because it's right at your fingertips.

Adjusting tension

So how do you know when the blade is tensioned correctly? It's really a matter of trial and error. Fine blades require less tension than thicker blades. Experienced scrollers often adjust tension and then pluck the blade with their finger (as shown in the middle photo) as if they were tuning the strings on a guitar. With experience, you'll be able to recognize the correct pitch or tone the blade makes when properly tensioned.

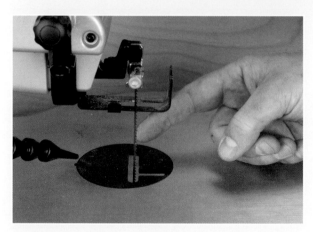

STRAIGHT BLADES PREVENT BREAKAGE

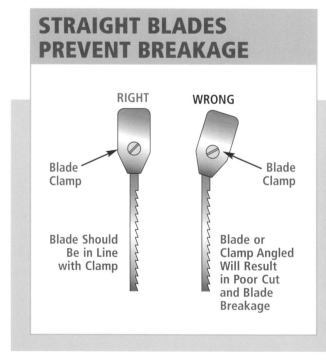

RIGHT   WRONG

Blade Clamp

Blade Clamp

Blade Should Be in Line with Clamp

Blade or Clamp Angled Will Result in Poor Cut and Blade Breakage

PREVENTING BLADE BREAKAGE

One of the most common causes of blade breakage is an improperly installed blade. The number one problem here is created when the blade is inserted crooked in the blade clamp. It's important to insert the blade so it's parallel to the jaws of the clamp pad, as shown in the bottom drawing. If the blade is installed at an angle, it will create excess stress where the blade enters the clamp, usually resulting in premature blade breakage.

Squaring the Table

After the blade is installed, it's a good idea to verify that the blade is perfectly perpendicular to the saw table. One quick way to check this is to gently butt the handle of a small square (like the engineer's square shown in the top photo) up against the blade. Squat down in front of the saw so your eyes are level with the table and see if there's any gap between the square and the blade, at either the top or bottom of the square. If there's no gap, you're ready to scroll.

When you do see a gap, you'll need to realign the table. On most saws, this means loosening a lock knob below the table top, as shown in the middle photo. Loosen the knob so it's just friction-tight. Then, holding the square in one hand, tap the table top as needed on one side or the other to eliminate any gap. Tighten the knob and recheck. Often the act of tightening the lock knob will cause the table to shift out of alignment. If this happens, readjust as necessary.

SIMPLE DYNAMIC TEST

Here's a quick way to check a table for square without using a try square. Start by making a shallow kerf on the edge of a board. Then rotate the workpiece with the same surface flat on the saw table so the kerf you just cut ends up behind the blade, as shown in the bottom photo. If the blade is aligned with the kerf, the table is square. If it isn't aligned, the table is out of square.

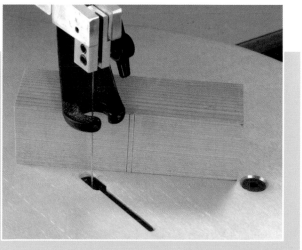

Safe Scrolling

Although the scroll saw is one of the safer tools in a workshop, there are still a number of comfort and safety issues. In terms of comfort, the two most common sources of fatigue are tables that are not set to the right height, and improper foot positioning.

Table working height

The distance the saw table is from the floor and your workshop stool or seat will have a major impact on how comfortable your scroll is to use—especially for periods of extended use. The generally accepted standard is to elevate the saw so the table is somewhere between 38" and 40" above the floor. This puts the table at a height that should be slightly higher than your elbows when you're sitting at the saw, as shown in the top drawing. If you notice that your neck or shoulders are cramping, try adjusting the table height up or down. With a little trial and error here, you should be able to pinpoint the exact height that works best for you.

Foot position

Folks who study ergonomics have proven that when seated for long periods at a workstation or work-bench, it helps some people to have their feet resting on an angled surface. This takes some of the pressure off the knees and spinal column. You can angle your feet simply by resting them on the inside lip of the saw cabinet, as shown in the middle photo. Alternatively, you can rest them on a couple of bricks, scrap wood...whatever you have lying around that can be used to elevate the toes.

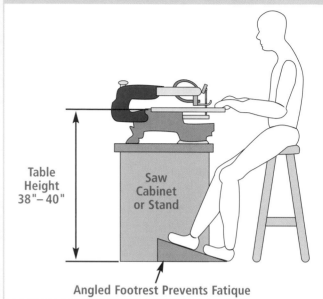

TABLE WORKING HEIGHT

Table Height 38"– 40"

Saw Cabinet or Stand

Angled Footrest Prevents Fatique

SHOP-MADE ANGLED FOOTREST

The scroll saw stand featured on pages 123–128 has a built-in footrest. Even if you don't build the stand, you can adapt the footrest to your saw cabinet or stand. The footrest is basically just a pair of wood scraps that are connected with a piano hinge; they attach to the front lip of the cabinet via another piano hinge, as shown in the bottom photo. Hinging the pieces allows you to lay them flat in the cabinet bottom if desired.

DEALING WITH DUST

When most woodworkers think about controlling dust in the workshop, they usually envision a large collector hooked up to the big dust-producing machines, like the table saw or planer, with pipes and hoses. Rarely does the image of a scroll saw come to mind. That's because scroll saws aren't big dust-producers—but you still need to be concerned about the dust. The super-fine dust that a scroll saw produces when cutting is just the stuff to worry about. Because your head is usually positioned close to the blade so you can see the line of cut, you're in position to breathe in a lot of fine dust. This is why it's so important to do what you can to control the dust that the saw produces.

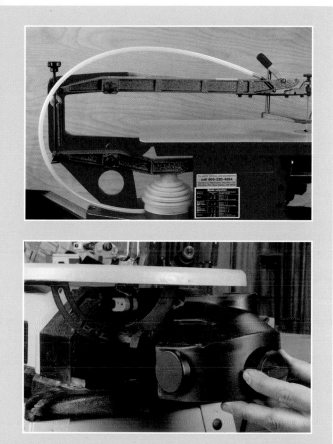

Built-in blowers. Beginning scrollers often think that a built-in blower equals dust collection. It doesn't. The built-in blower like the one shown in the top photo is designed purely to blow the dust away from the surface that you're cutting so you can more easily see the line you're trying to follow. While convenient, this does in fact disperse the dust in a cloud around your head. If you're not planning on any other kind of dust control, at least wear a dust mask to keep this dust out of your lungs.

Collection box. Although not really dust control, the collection box on some saws (like the one shown in the middle photo) does a pretty good job of keeping your saw clean. And if the dust isn't falling onto the saw base or floor, then it's less likely to end up in your lungs. If your saw has a box like this, make sure to empty it before you start a new project.

Vacuum ports. The best way to control the dust that a scroll saw produces is to suck it away with a vacuum. Some savvy saw manufacturers have designed built-in vacuum ports (like the one shown in the bottom photo) that, when hooked up to your shop vacuum, will whisk away harmful dust. Since most dust ports hook up under the table—and the saw teeth point down—most of the dust is collected.

Adjusting Hold-Downs & Blade Guards

Once a blade is installed in the saw, there are a couple of simple adjustments you'll need to make before you can begin cutting: on the hold-down and on the blade guard.

Hold-downs

A hold-down is designed to keep the workpiece pressed firmly against the table top and prevent chatter (top left photo). The hold-down itself may be either stout or flexible; many experienced scrollers prefer a flexible hold-down, because they find it easier and quicker to adjust. In most cases, the hold-down itself is connected to a rod that fits into a clamp on either side of the saw frame (top right photo). The hold-down may be rubber or metal. What side the adjustment is on will affect how easy it is to use. If you're a lefty, look for an adjustment on the left side—it'll just be more convenient.

Since you'll be constantly adjusting your hold-down to compensate for different thicknesses of wood, it's important that it be easy to use and lock positively once in place. Some manufacturers recommend simply loosening the hold-down lock knob and letting the hold-down drop onto the work surface, and then tightening the knob. Although this permits a quick adjustment, it tends to put too much pressure on the workpiece, making it difficult to feed into the saw blade.

Blade guards

Blade guards vary in design from saw to saw; their purpose is to keep your fingers from contacting the blade when making a cut. There is no perfect blade guard, so it's still up to you to keep your fingers away from the blade. Two-pronged guards (like the

one shown in the bottom left photo) provide some safety but can still allow a finger to slip between the prongs. Other guards (like the post-style guard in the bottom right photo) do a good job of preventing contact head-on, but don't offer much protection from the side. Regardless of what type of guard your saw has, it can't do its job if it is not used or not adjusted properly. Make sure to read and follow the adjustment procedure in the owner's manual.

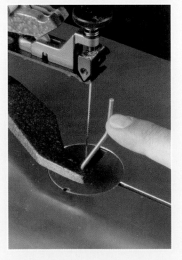

Speed and Feed Rates

Most modern scroll saws come equipped with variable-speed motors. However, there are only a few occasions when you will actually need to change speeds.

Speed

For the most part, you want to use the highest speed your saw is capable of running at, since this will provide the smoothest cut.

The only times you'll need to lower the speed are when cutting into tough materials like metal and composites, plastics, and some exotic woods such as ebony or rosewood. Slow speeds also work best for cutting veneers, as they give greater control while minimizing the risk of grabbing and snapping the fragile material.

Feed rate

Smooth, problem-free cuts have less to do with how fast the motor is running than they do a proper feed rate—that is, the speed at which the workpiece is fed into the saw blade. Finding the best feed rate for a specific material is a matter of trial and error (bottom photo). How the blade cuts and the sound the saw makes are two indicators that can help you find the proper rate.

If you notice that the saw blade is bowing excessively as you press the workpiece in for a cut, you're feeding too fast. This also tends to overheat the blade and will eventually result in breakage. If you see discoloration on the blade (as shown in the inset photo), you've been feeding the workpiece too fast. This can also leave rough edges and create a lot of tearout. If you're feeding the workpiece too slow, the blade can actually rub against the edge enough to create sufficient friction to burn the wood. Just increase the feed rate and this should disappear (as long as the blade is still sharp). Finally, the sound the motor makes can help you identify correct feed rates. If the pitch lowers significantly during a cut, you're bogging down the motor and the feed rate is too fast.

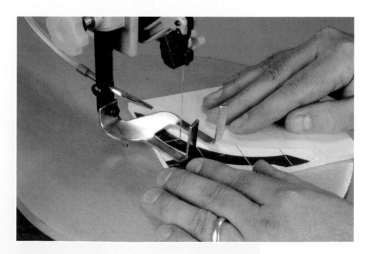

Basic Technique

Most scrolling means following a pattern. How well you can follow a line depends on your eye/hand coordination, but can also be affected by variables such as the type of blade you're using, the wood you're cutting, and being aware of the blade's natural tendencies to follow the grain.

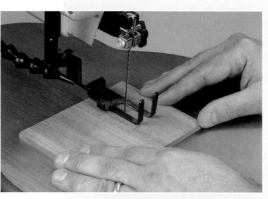

Straight cuts

Depending on the type of wood, its thickness, and the blade you're using, straight cuts can be either difficult or easy. Woods with little pronounced grain, and engineered woods like plywood, particleboard, and hardboard, are easy to make controlled cuts in. For woods where the grain is pronounced—like oak—it can be a real challenge to make a straight cut, as the blade will have a tendency to follow the grain.

At the same time, the blade itself may be creating problems for you. That's because most scroll saw blades are milled, and the resulting burr that forms on one side of the blade tends to pull the workpiece to either side. This tendency to pull to one side is called drift. To find out if your blade "drifts," mark a straight line on a scrap workpiece and feed it gently into the running blade as shown in the top photo. Take care not to redirect the workpiece if it starts cutting off the line. If it does, stop about halfway through the cut and use a pencil to draw a light line on your table top to indicate the angle of drift. This way you can compensate and make other straight cuts by aligning the new workpiece to this marked angle, as shown in the middle photo.

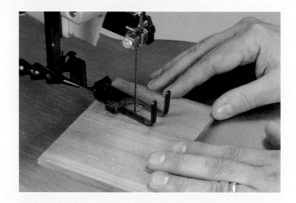

Starting and ending cuts

How you start a cut into a workpiece can affect how easy or hard it is to follow the pattern. Whenever you start with the grain, you run the risk of the blade following the grain. In most cases, you'll find it easier to control if you start your cuts against the grain, as shown in the bottom drawing.

GRAIN DIRECTION AND STARTING POINT

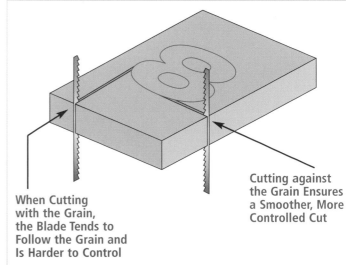

When Cutting with the Grain, the Blade Tends to Follow the Grain and Is Harder to Control

Cutting against the Grain Ensures a Smoother, More Controlled Cut

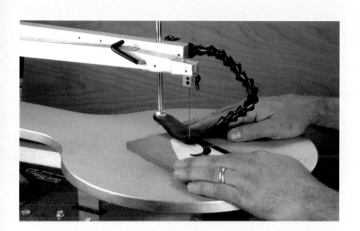

Curved Cuts

Cutting curves is what a scroll saw is all about. To make a curved cut, guide the workpiece with both hands as shown in the top photo. There are a couple of different techniques you can use to make the cut in one motion. With one method, you leave one hand fixed and push the edge of the workpiece with the other to pivot the workpiece into the blade. This will create a smooth, flowing curve. The problem is, it's hard to know when to pivot the workpiece—only time spent at the saw will help you develop this skill. The other method is to keep both hands moving to guide the workpiece and make the cut. This is more common but generally produces a rougher curve.

Splitting the line

Most of the time when you're following a pattern, you should try to either split the pattern line with the saw blade or stay just a hair to the waste side (inset photo). Staying to the waste side of the line lets you come back with a sanding stick or file later and sand or file exactly to the line. In most scrollwork this isn't necessary, as what you're after is a smooth line that closely approximates the pattern.

Correcting mistakes gradually

Mistakes are going to occur when you scroll: It's inevitable. Whether the blade inadvertently follows the grain or your attention strays for a second, you'll drift off of your pattern line. When this happens, what you want to avoid is the knee-jerk reaction of correcting immediately (bottom drawing). When you do this, the mistake will be obvious—usually in the form of a bump or ridge. What you want to do is gradually steer the blade back on track to create a smooth transition. This will look less like a mistake and more like the original pattern shape.

CORRECTING MISTAKES GRADUALLY

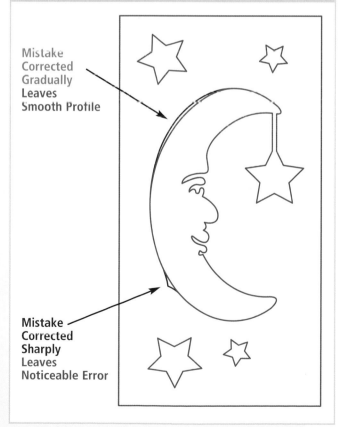

Mistake Corrected Gradually Leaves Smooth Profile

Mistake Corrected Sharply Leaves Noticeable Error

"Filing" with a blade

One technique every experienced scroller has picked up over time is to use a blade as a file to clean up cuts and remove bumps or ridges. This requires a light touch but can be very useful. To file with a blade, gently push the workpiece into the blade at the point where you want to clean up—if necessary, wiggle the workpiece from side to side to help file a smooth transition, as shown in the top photo.

CUTTING CORNERS

Many of the scroll cuts you'll make will be 90-degree corners. There are a couple of methods to create a sharp inter-section of the two lines, depending on whether it's an inside corner or an outside corner.

Inside corners. The two ways to make an inside corner cut are to come into the corner from both sides with two separate cuts, or by backtracking (middle drawing). The two-cut method is simpler, but often not feasible with a pierced cut. With backtracking, you cut into the corner, backtrack a bit, cut a tight radius to intersect the adjacent line, and then cut into the corner to form a sharp intersection.

Outside corners. The simplest way to cut an outside corner is with two cuts, each cutting through to the edges of the workpiece (bottom drawing). You can also backtrack in a manner similar to that used to cut an inside corner; the difference here is that the backtrack curve is on the outside of the corner versus the inside. Finally, an elegant method used by many experienced scrollers is to make a loop cut. This method allows you to make the corner in a single continuous cut.

METHODS OF CUTTING INSIDE CORNERS

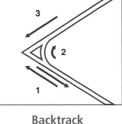

Two Cuts   Backtrack

METHODS OF CUTTING OUTSIDE CORNERS

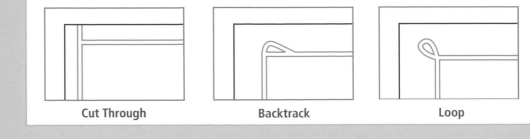

Cut Through   Backtrack   Loop

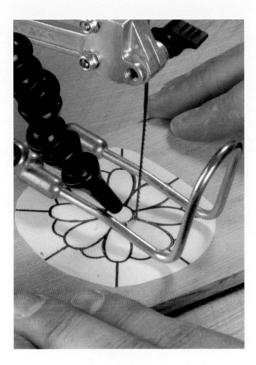

On-the-Spot Turns

One of the most amazing things you can do on a scroll saw—an on-the-spot turn—is impossible on any other power tool. The reason a scroll saw can do this is its narrow blade. The blade is so narrow that it can almost turn around inside the kerf it makes—almost. The secret to making an on-the-spot turn is to let the saw blade widen the kerf slightly where you'll be turning. This takes some getting used to, but it will become automatic with practice.

Here's how to make an on-the-spot turn. Grab a couple of scraps of wood and turn on the saw. Feed one piece into the blade until it reaches roughly the middle of the scrap. Then rotate the workpiece quickly in one direction or the other, see the drawing below. It doesn't really matter which direction—whichever works best for you. The idea here is to pivot the workpiece around the blade. As you rotate the workpiece, the blade will widen the kerf, letting you turn the workpiece in a complete circle if you like. What you're really doing here is "filing" a tiny hole for the blade, just as if you were filing away a bump or ridge as described on page 68.

Beginning scrollers have a tendency to rotate the workpiece too slowly, and the blade will file a large hole instead a small one. Continue practicing this valuable technique until you can effortlessly spin a workpiece around the blade. A good practice exercise is to lay out a five-pointed star and make on-the-spot turns on the points of the star. The better you get at this, the finer the points will be.

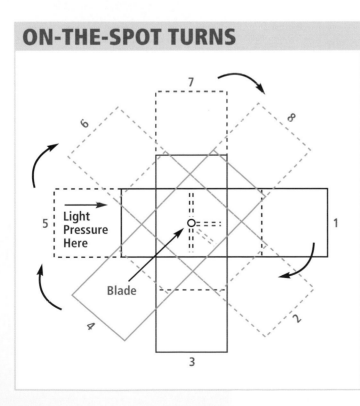

ON-THE-SPOT TURNS

Light Pressure Here

Blade

On-the-Spot Corners

A version of the on-the-spot turn is the on-the-spot corner. The difference here is that you'll be making just a 90-degree turn versus a 180 or even a 360, see the drawing below. Although it may sound easier than making an on-the-spot-turn, an on-the-spot corner can be a real challenge: If you rotate too far, it's easy to spin the workpiece past the intersecting line and into the pattern itself.

Like so many techniques, this one can be mastered only with a lot of practice. Since on-the-spot corners are used widely for making pierced-cut squares, draw a set of varying-size squares on a scrap piece and start practicing.

You'll find that one of the secrets to successful on-the-spot corners is to keep just a slight pressure on the workpiece on the side opposite the one you're pivoting. This helps to both control the spin and keep the point of the intersection sharp.

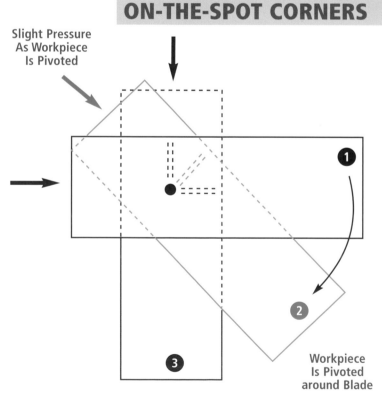

ON-THE-SPOT CORNERS

Slight Pressure As Workpiece Is Pivoted

1

2

3

Workpiece Is Pivoted around Blade

Making Clean Cuts

In a perfect world, every cut you made on a scroll saw would be clean, smooth, and splinter-free. There'd be no chip-out and no tear-out, and no sanding would be required. In the not-so-perfect world this doesn't happen. Virtually every cut you make will create some splintering or tear-out. There are, however, a number of techniques you can use to minimize this.

Use reverse-tooth blades

Splintering on the scroll saw usually occurs as the blades exits the workpiece on the downstroke. To prevent this, the reverse-tooth blade was developed. On this specialty blade, a number of teeth on the bottom of the blade are reversed so that they cut on the upstroke (inset photo). For this type of blade to work, you may have to modify the blade to match the thickness of the workpiece. Reverse-tooth blades work best with one to two teeth showing above the table top on the upstroke. You may need to adjust the position of the blade in the clamps or even trim some length off the blade for this to occur. If the reverse teeth pass all the way though the workpiece, they'll splinter the top of the workpiece as they exit—just the opposite problem of a standard blade.

Keep the kerf clear

Another common cause of rough cuts is sawdust trapped in the saw kerf. This can lead to burning and chip-out. The solution is to back up as needed to keep the kerf clear of dust, as shown in the middle photo.

Tape to prevent tear-out

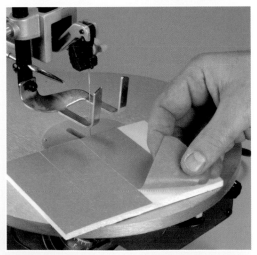

A final way to prevent tear-out and splintering is to apply masking tape to the bottom of your workpiece as shown in the bottom photo. The masking tape helps supports the wood fibers as the blade exits the workpiece, keeping splintering to a minimum.

Working with Plastic

Plastic cuts easily on the scroll saw. The only challenge is finding the correct combination of speed and feed rate.

Slower speed

Choose a slower speed for cutting into most plastics. Higher speeds tend to melt the plastic instead of cutting it. This is particularly true with acrylics, where the parts tend to fuse back together after they've been cut. Blade speeds between 600 and 800 strokes per minute will work best for most plastics. Additionally, consider covering the top of the plastic with duct tape. This will help dissipate heat and prevent the parts from fusing back together.

Finding the feed rate

The only way to find the correct feed rate for cutting into plastic is to experiment with scraps before cutting into your project material. If you're using a slower speed and the parts fuse together like those shown in the middle photo, you need to slow down the feed rate. This is just a matter of trial and error until you find the correct combination. You'll know that you've found it when the parts cut cleanly and stay separate.

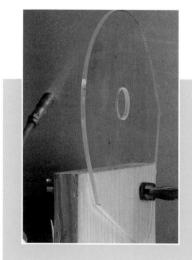

HEAT-TREATING EDGES

Even when cut with a fine-tooth scroll saw blade, the sawn edges of plastic can be rough and show saw marks. These are easy to remove by flame-treating the edges. In effect, all you're doing is melting the plastic edge enough to melt away the ridges so it flows to create a smooth edge. A propane torch commonly used to sweat copper pipe works great for this. Make sure to direct the flame only at the edges and keep it moving to prevent the plastic from catching fire.

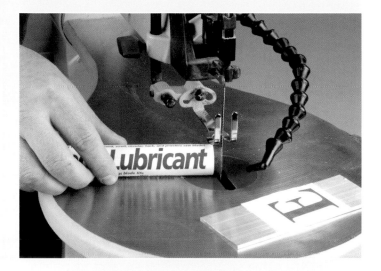

Working with Metal

Many metals are surprisingly easy to cut on the scroll saw to make jewelry, accents, and decorations like holiday ornaments. Sheet brass, copper, and aluminum all cut well, as long as you use a metal-cutting blade and a high speed.

Use a lubricant

Most metals will cut faster and cleaner if you use some form of lubricant. Special lubricant sticks like the one shown in the top photo are available just for this purpose, but paste wax or even an old crayon will work fine. Apply the lubricant directly to the blade with the power off. Another way to keep the blade lubricated is to apply paste wax to the bottom of backer board used when cutting thin stock (see below). This not only keeps the blade lubricated, but it also helps the workpiece slide freely on the table top as you make your cuts.

Sandwich thin stock

If you're planning on cutting thin sheet stock, it's best to either sandwich the metal between two thin layers of wood as shown in the middle photo, or at the very least bond the metal to a bottom backer board with spray adhesive. Either of these methods helps prevent the metal from reciprocating with the blade—a tendency it will have if cut alone—and also prevents the metal from scratching your table top.

Cutting thicker stock

Thicker stock, like the aluminum bar stock shown in the bottom photo, can be effectively sawn without a backer board. Again, though, it's still a good idea to use a bottom backer just to prevent table-top scratches. Keep in mind that many metals—in both bar and sheet form—often have a protective coating sprayed on top to retard tarnishing. You may find it necessary to remove this to get a pattern to stick to the metal successfully. Steel wool or an abrasive pad dipped in acetone or mineral spirits will usually do the job.

Sanding

While this tool is called a scroll saw, did you know it can also scroll-sand? All it takes to turn your scroll saw into a power scroll sander is the right sanding accessory. You can purchase these or make your own; see the sidebar below.

Sanding accessory

Most mail-order woodworking catalogs and scroll saw manufacturers sell a sanding accessory for the scroll saw. These disposable sanding "blades" are nothing more than strips of sandpaper similar to the kind used on belt sanders. The sanders are fitted with plastic end tabs that can be gripped by the saw's clamp pads (top photo). Installing one of these is as simple as changing a blade. Once it's installed, apply enough tension to pull the strip taut, while still allowing it to flex a bit in use.

MAKE YOUR OWN SANDING BLADES

If you want to power-sand but don't want to special-order sanding strips, you can make your own from ordinary emery boards. The only thing to keep in mind when shopping for these is that the board needs to be at least 5" long or you won't be able to mount it in your saw.

Emery board. Trim an ordinary emery board to length to fit between the clamp pads of your saw. They're easy to trim with scissors or diagonal cutters, as shown here.

Mount in saw. To mount the emery board, you may need to widen the gap between the clamp pads. Then insert the board and clamp it in place.

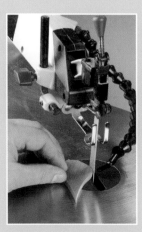

Power sanding. Use steady, even pressure to power-sand a part. When the grit on the board begins to wear out, you can flip the board end-for-end or rotate it to present a fresh sanding surface.

Cleaning Up Cuts

In addition to power-sanding a cut clean, there are a number of elbow-grease-powered sanding and shaping tools that will also do a great job: sanding sticks, needle files and rasps, and riflers.

Sanding sticks

One specialty tool that many scrollers find extremely useful for cleaning up cuts is the sanding stick. These sticks are small, spring-loaded plastic frames that accept narrow sanding belts, as shown in the top photo. The sanding frame is curved on one end and pointed on the other to access even the most delicate detail. As the sanding belt dulls, all you have to do is rotate it to present a fresh sanding surface. Belt grits come in fine, medium, and coarse.

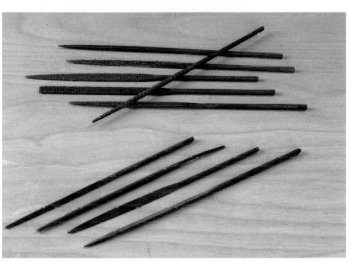

Needle files and rasps

Needle files (sometimes called jeweler's files) are thin, delicate files that are used for small, fine detail work. They're usually sold in sets that include a variety of shapes, including round (often called a rat-tail file), square, rectangular, half-round, triangular, and flat (middle photo). Their diminutive size makes them ideal for fitting into delicate pierced cuts to fine-tune a detail. Needle rasps have the same ability to fit into tight spaces, only they can remove material much faster.

Riflers

Riflers are specialty files used primarily by carvers to smooth out small details in their work. These may be double-ended or come with a handle as shown in the bottom photo. Riflers are available individually or in sets and can be either files or rasps. Like needle files, they can reach into small spaces; but because they are larger and have handles, riflers generally offer more control.

Working with Small Parts

Some of the scroll projects you'll want to tackle will call for scroll cuts to be made on small parts. You can try and cut these as you would any other part, but you'll bring your fingers dangerously close to the blade. Here are three techniques you can use to cut small parts safely.

Start with an oversized blank

The first method for working with small parts may seem a bit obvious, but it's often overlooked—start with an oversized blank, as shown in the top photo. As you make your cuts, make sure to leave a "handle" or two on the small part until you're almost finished scrolling. Then use the handle to guide the work-piece past the blade to separate the small part.

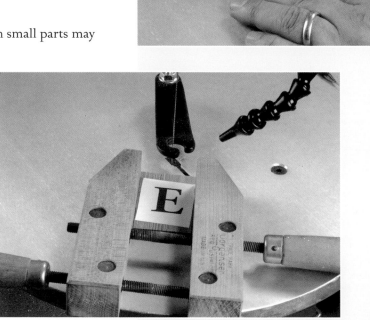

Use a clamp

If for any reason you must work with a small part, consider holding it with a clamp as shown in the middle photo. Small wood handscrews like the one shown work well for this, since their square jaws can firmly grip the edges of the workpiece. Your best bet with this method is to make pierced cuts: This will leave the surrounding waste portion of the blank intact so the clamp jaws can grip it without crushing it.

Attach workpiece to a sled

The final method for cutting small parts is to attach the small part to a scrapwood "sled" or backer board, as shown in the bottom photo. This keeps your fingers well away from the saw blade. As with using an oversized blank, you'll need to leave a "handle" on the sled to let you finish scrolling before cutting the part free, as described above.

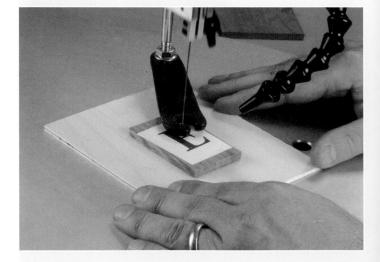

Cutting Thin Stock

Working with thin stock takes a lot of care and patience. That's because the fragile stock you're cutting easily fractures, splits, or breaks. Fortunately, there are a number of things you can do to reduce the chances of this happening.

Reduce the table opening

To make cutting thin stock easier, one of the simplest things you can do is to fully support the stock around the blade as it scrolls up and down. One way to do this is to replace the standard table insert with a "zero-clearance" insert, as shown in the top photo. Reducing the opening like this can mean all the difference between a successful cut and disaster.

If you don't have a replaceable insert like this, you can do the next best thing, which is to make a zero-clearance top for your table. All this requires is a scrap of thin plywood slightly larger than your table top. Just feed it into the blade until the front edge is parallel to your table top, shut off the saw, and clamp it to the top as shown in the middle photo.

Sandwich cut

Another way to support thin stock is to sandwich it between two pieces of stiffer stock and then make the cut, as shown in the bottom photo. Additionally, slow down the speed of the saw and try to press down the top layer as near the blade as possible while still keeping a safe distance away.

Scrolling Thick Stock

Although most scrollwork projects involve cutting stock that's 3/4" thick or less, you'll occasionally find it necessary to scroll thicker stock. Most scroll saws can handle stock up to 1¹/₂" in thickness. To cut thick stock successfully, you'll need to tweak your saw a bit.

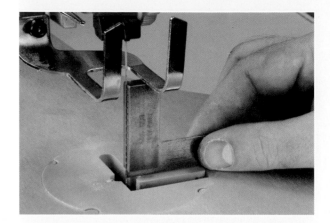

Square the table
One of the leading causes of problems when cutting thick stock is a table top that's not perpendicular to the saw blade. This creates an angled cut in thick stock, which just makes the saw work harder and puts the blade under unnecessary stress. Take the time to check the blade with a small square as shown in the top photo, and adjust the table as necessary.

Increase blade tension
Another problem you're likely to encounter when cutting thick stock is the blade bowing to one side or the other. This is called a "barrel" cut and can often be prevented by increasing the blade tension (middle photo). In some cases, this won't prevent barreling, but it will reduce it.

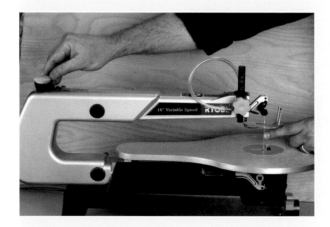

THICK-STOCK BLADES

The big challenge when cutting thick stock is that it's virtually impossible for gullets between the saw teeth to ferry away the sawdust from the kerf. That's because so many of the teeth are completely contained within the stock since it's so thick. One way to prevent this is to use special "thick-stock" blades (bottom photo). These special blades have teeth with a wide set to create a wider kerf. This prevents sawdust from building up and creating frictional heat, which can both burn the wood and overheat the blade.

MAKING STACKED CUTS

Because some of the scrolling projects you'll want to make have duplicate parts, it's logical to cut these in batches, if possible. A common way to duplicate parts made with thin stock is to simply stack them on top of one another and cut them all at once. Here are three ways to secure the blanks together for making stacked cuts.

Double-sided tape. The most reliable way to secure stacked blanks for cutting is to insert double-sided tape between the parts, as shown in the top photo. Take care to tape the entire area that's to be scrolled to prevent parts from working loose. If you find it difficult to separate the parts after you've made your cuts, drizzle a little lacquer thinner into the joints; this will dissolve the glue so you can separate the parts with ease.

Brads. Another method for securing blanks together is to tack them together with brads, as shown in the middle photo. This has the disadvantage of leaving small brad holes in the parts, but these can easily be filled with wood putty. Take care to keep the brads away from the line of cut so you won't accidentally hit one and ruin your blade.

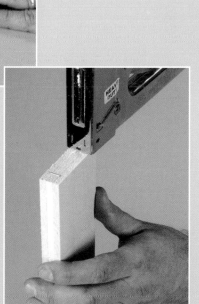

Staples on edges. Finally, you can hold blanks together by stapling them together on the edges, as shown in the bottom photo. This works best for parts that require pierced cuts, since once you cut past the edges, there's nothing to hold the parts together.

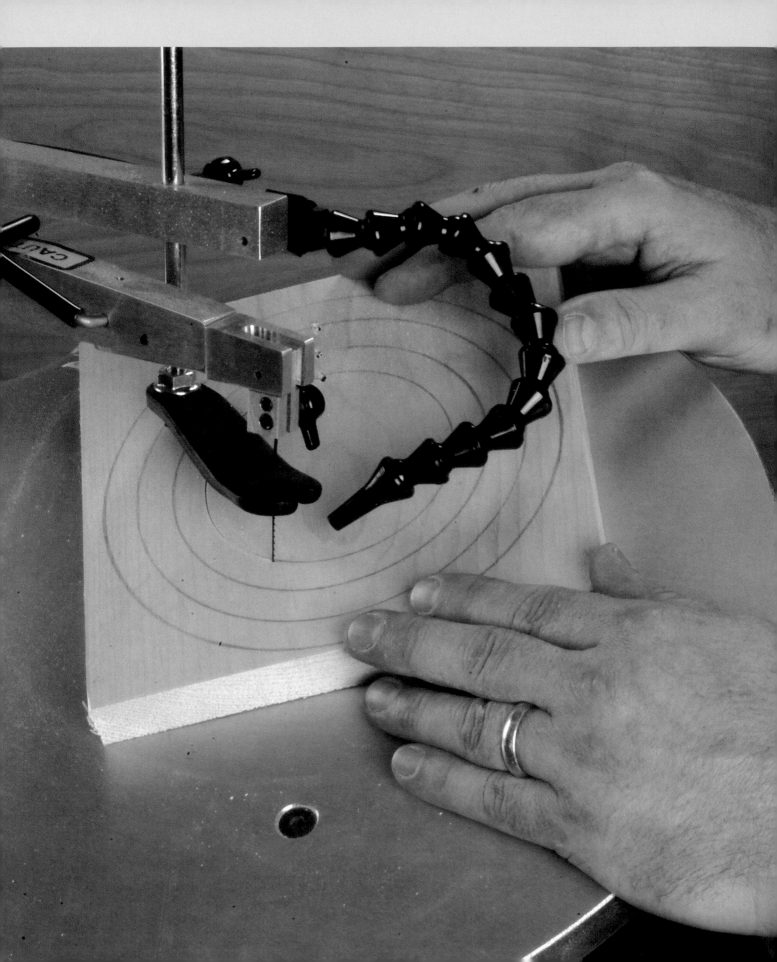

4 Advanced Scroll Saw Techniques

The scroll saw has long been an underrated shop tool. It has a reputation for use only to make fancy scrollwork: silhouettes, puzzles, shelves, displays, etc. But with a little knowledge, you can use a scroll saw regularly on all types of projects. There are two reasons for this. First, a scroll saw can make pierced cuts (cuts in from the edge of a workpiece)—something a band saw can't handle. Second, with the proper blade, the cut that's left by a scroll saw is amazingly smooth. Combine these and you have a tool that can solve a lot of problems.

This chapter advances beyond the basics. You'll see how to bevel-saw and chamfer with the scroll saw, and how to make concentric rings and collapsible baskets. Additional advanced techniques include compound sawing, fretwork, intarsia, overlays, marquetry, and even joinery. After learning the techniques in this chapter, you'll wonder how you ever got along without a scroll saw in the shop.

Did you know you could make a bowl with a scroll saw? And not just a round one: how about a heart-shaped bowl, or an oval basket? You can make almost any size or shape bowl or basket using the concentric-rings technique shown here.

Bevel-Sawing

As with most other stationary tools, cutting at an angle on the scroll saw is accomplished by first tilting the table. What's different about the scroll saw is that you'll often be bevel-sawing curves and tight radii—and these can be tricky if you don't know how to handle them. Here, you'll find guidelines on basic technique, and then see how to make cones and even chamfer edges.

Adjusting the table angle

The bevel indicators on most tilting tables are not very reliable. In most cases, it's best to check the angle with a protractor or adjustable triangle. Unfortunately, neither of these work well with the scroll saw because there's little if any clearance between the top arm of the saw and the table when it's tilted. A simple solution is to accurately cut a scrap piece to the desired angle and then use this as a visual aid to set the table angle, as shown in the top photo.

Basic technique

Once you've set the table angle and locked it in place, you can begin cutting. As always, you'll want to try to split the pattern line or stay just slightly to the waste side of the line. The thing to remember when bevel-sawing is that you're removing more wood than if you were cutting at 90 degrees. That's because the distance between the surfaces of the wood is longer at an angle than straight at 90 degrees. With this in mind, you'll want to slow down your feed rate to match the cutting ability of the blade. And because you'll be generating more dust, it's important to keep the kerf clean. Stop frequently and blow the dust out of the kerf.

Cutting inside corners

Something you may not think of until you try it is what happens when you cut inside corners. Unlike 90-degree cuts, you won't get a clean, sharp corner. If you make two separate cuts, you'll end up with kerfed edges as shown in the drawing below. Eliminate these by making an on-the-spot turn (see page 83). This technique will eliminate kerfs, but it leaves one corner sharp and the other rounded (bottom drawing).

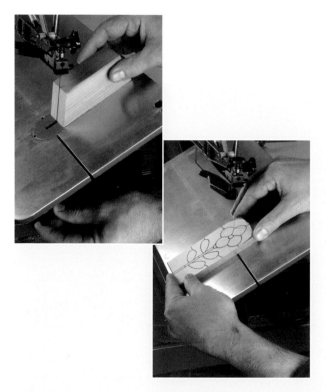

BEVELING CORNERS

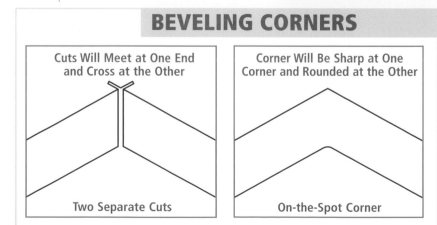

Cuts Will Meet at One End and Cross at the Other	Corner Will Be Sharp at One Corner and Rounded at the Other
Two Separate Cuts	On-the-Spot Corner

BEVELING: ON-THE-SPOT TURNS

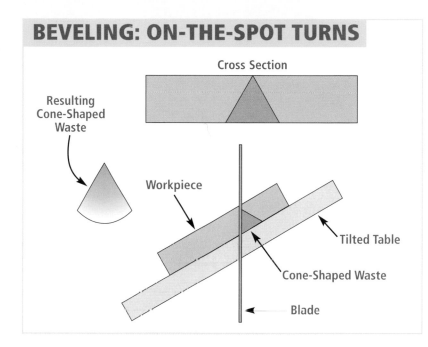

Cross Section

Resulting Cone-Shaped Waste

Workpiece

Tilted Table

Cone-Shaped Waste

Blade

On-the-spot turns

When you need to make an on-the-spot turn while bevel-sawing, the thing to keep in mind is that you're removing a lot more wood than if it were a 90-degree turn. Again, the secret to a successful turn is to slow down your feed rate to let the blade plow through the extra thickness. If you make a complete 360-degree on-the-spot turn, you'll end up with a cone-shaped waste piece, as shown in the drawing at left.

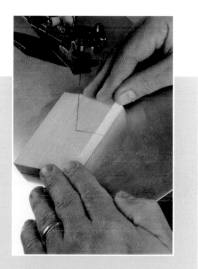

MAKING CONES

The cones that result from making 360-degree on-the-spot turns can be used as decorative accents or decorations on many of your woodworking projects. They make excellent Christmas trees and can also be used as trees for hobbies like model-making and for decorating landscapes for model railroads. You can make tall, skinny ones by using thick stock and a low angle, or short, fat ones with thinner stock and high angles.

Rotate the workpiece. To make a cone, adjust the table to the desired angle and slowly feed the workpiece into the blade. Stop, and then begin rotating the workpiece, keeping the blade in the same position. You're basically rotating the workpiece around the blade. Continue rotating until you're back to your starting point.

Remove the cone. When you've completed the cut, you can do one of two things: Either stop the saw and remove the cone, or try to back the workpiece off the blade by backtracking through your original kerf. Experienced scrollers tend to backtrack out, but if you're a novice scroller, you'll find it easier to stop the saw. If you don't, the blade can come in contact with the cone—which has been freed from the workpiece and will bounce around—and damage the surface of the cone.

CHAMFERING

The scroll saw can tackle chamfering tasks that other tools can't handle. That's because you can select any chamfer angle you want just by tilting the table. The angles on chamfering router bits are set at either 45 or 30 degrees. Not only can you adjust the scroll chamfer to any angle, but you can also vary the depth of cut easily to create a sculpted or scalloped edge. There are two ways to chamfer on the scroll saw: freehand and using a fence.

Freehand. To chamfer freehand on the scroll saw, start by tilting the table to the desired angle. If you're looking for a uniform chamfer, first use a pencil to draw the chamfer around the perimeter of the workpiece on its face and edge. Second, practice first—it takes a steady hand to get a uniform chamfer. If uniformity is what you're after, consider using a fence as described below. Ease the edge of the workpiece into the blade and rotate as needed to cut the chamfer, as shown in the top photo.

Chamfering with a fence. You'll find it easier to create a more uniform chamfer on the scroll saw if you use a fence as a guide. To do this, temporarily clamp a wood scrap to the saw's table. Position it away from the blade the desired depth of cut, as shown in the bottom left photo.

To cut a chamfer, ease the edge of the workpiece into the blade until it contacts the fence. Then rotate the workpiece, taking care to keep the uncut edge of the workpiece at a tangent to the fence directly opposite the blade, as shown in the bottom right photo. If you vary where the workpiece touches the fence, you'll end up with an uneven chamfer. It's best to practice on a scrap piece before cutting into your project stock.

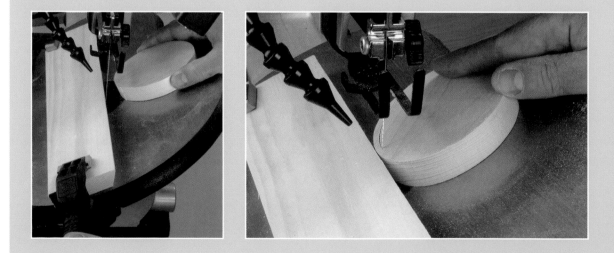

Cutting Relief Designs

The original relief designs made with a scroll saw were probably an accident. The scroller unknowingly left the saw table at a slight angle and cut out a picture or a puzzle, only to find that the pieces wouldn't come out cleanly. Because of the angle, the parts would wedge against each other and only come out partially—and the very first relief design was created (top photo).

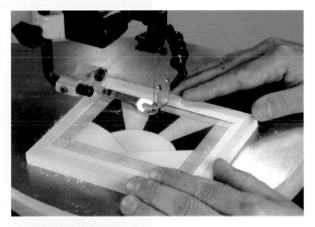

Make bevel cuts

To make a relief design, start by attaching a pattern to a blank and then set the saw table for a slight angle. Three degrees will do nicely for most work—the steeper the angle, the more the parts will protrude; the lower the angle, the less they'll extend out. Drill access holes and start cutting out the design as shown in the middle photo. Remember that you are bevel-sawing and so will be making a heavier cut; slow down your feed rate and let the blade cut at its own speed.

Raise sections and apply glue

When all the parts are cut out, push from the back of the design to make the desired portions protrude. Once in place, secure the pieces together with glue as shown in the bottom photo. Hot-melt glue works best for this because it bridges gaps (the kerfs) well and sets up quickly. You'll find that you can get even more 3-D effect by varying how far out each piece protrudes.

Cutting Concentric Rings

One of the coolest things you can do with the bevel-sawing technique is to make a bowl from a single flat board. How? By cutting concentric rings and gluing the segments back together. This gets around one of the negative aspects of most bowl turning—wasting wood. When a typical bowl is turned on a lathe, the interior of the bowl is scooped out with a gouge—all that good wood ends up as shavings. But with a concentric-ring bowl, there is no waste. The trick is to lay out the bowl shape on paper first to make sure the rings will align, as shown in the top drawing. Then simply set your saw table to match the angle you chose.

Drill angled access holes

To cut the concentric rings, you need to drill access holes, as these are pierced cuts. The difference here is that these holes must be drilled at an angle to match the angle of the bowl sides. The best tool for this job is the drill press: Just angle the table and drill. Alternatively, you can use a portable drill and a drilling guide, as shown in the middle photo. The guide shown is just a scrap of wood cut to match the desired cutting angle. Note that unless you have really long drill bits, or use a thin guide, the guide can only be used to start the hole a ways before the chuck hits the guide block. When this happens, remove the guide and finish the hole freehand.

Cut the first ring

Set the table to the desired angle and thread the blade through the innermost access hole. Turn on the saw and begin cutting the first ring as shown in the bottom photo. Take it slow, as you're removing a lot of wood. Rotate the workpiece smoothly and remember to correct any mistakes gradually to keep from creating bumps on the rings. Because the inner ring—which is actually the bottom of the bowl—is the smallest piece, it's safest to cut this first and work your way out toward the wider rings.

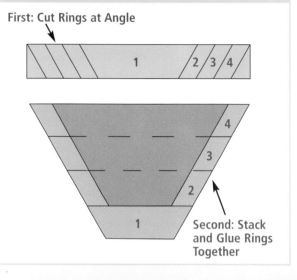

CONCENTRIC RINGS

First: Cut Rings at Angle

Second: Stack and Glue Rings Together

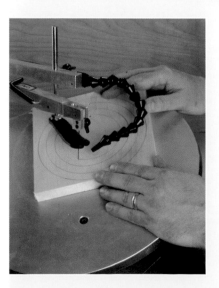

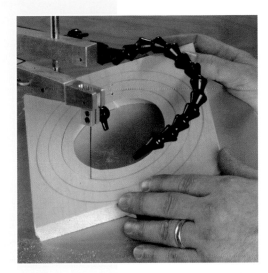

Continue cutting rings

After you've cut out the bottom of the bowl, stop the saw and release the blade. Thread it up through the next closest angled access hole and cut the next ring, as shown in the top photo. Repeat this process until all the rings have been cut out.

Glue up rings

Once everything is cut, you can glue up the segments to form the bowl blank. Apply a light coat of glue to mating surfaces, and stack the parts in order. Apply clamps as shown in the middle photo, and allow the blank to dry overnight. If you find it difficult to clamp all the segments together at once, consider gluing up two at a time and then gluing these pairs together. Many woodworkers find that this technique reduces the slipping and sliding that frequently occurs when gluing together multiple pieces.

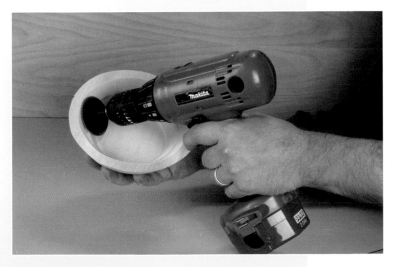

Turn or sand the bowl smooth

When the bowl blank is completely dry, you can smooth the exterior and interior. If you have a lathe, attach the blank to a screw or scroll chuck or baseplate and use a spindle or bowl-turning gouge to clean up and shape the sides and bottom. Alternatively, you can simply sand the surfaces smooth with sandpaper or sanding disks. The flexible sanding disk shown in the bottom photo is designed specifically for sanding bowls, and can be found in most mail-order woodworking catalogs.

COLLAPSIBLE BASKETS

The final bevel-sawing technique explained here is very specialized, and a big favorite: making collapsible baskets. This technique is similar to cutting concentric rings (pages 86–87), except instead of making separate angled rings, you make one single, long, continuous angled cut. This creates a "string" that wraps around to form the sides of the basket, much like a coiled pot made from clay. A separate handle attaches to the basket; when lifted up and placed on a cleat attached to the bottom of the basket, this creates the elegant piece shown in the top photo. When not in use, the handle is pivoted down to release the sides and the basket collapses flat for efficient storage. (For complete plans and step-by-step instructions on how to make a collapsible basket, see pages 182–184.)

One continuous bevel cut. The sides of a collapsible basket are formed by making a single, continuous angled cut. Just like relief designs, an angle around 3 degrees works well. Adjust your saw table and apply the basket pattern to

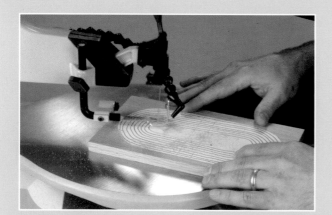

your blank. Start making your cut into the blank; once you begin cutting the "sides," take care to use a slow feed rate and a steady hand. Any variations in wall thickness will affect how easily the basket pops up into basket form, as well as how easily it collapses. When you've completed the cut, stop the saw, release the blade, and remove the workpiece.

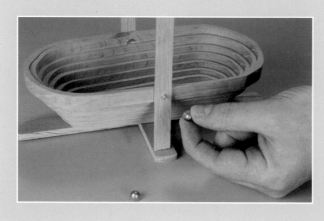

Assemble the basket. Once the basket is cut to shape, you'll need to make a pair of cleats for the bottom and attach them to the bottom of the basket. You'll also need a handle. The one shown here in the bottom photo was made by gluing up thin strips around a bending form. It creates a sturdy handle that won't split over time. Finally, use a pair of brass machine screws and nuts to secure the handle to the outermost "ring" of the basket.

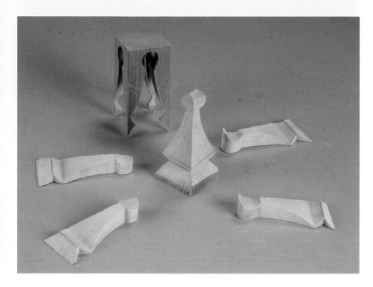

Compound Sawing

When most woodworkers think of compound sawing, they think of cutting crown molding on a miter saw or making complex cuts on the table saw using a tilted blade and an angled miter gauge. But compound sawing on the scroll saw doesn't involve any angled cutting at all. Instead, two sets of cuts are made on adjoining sides of a workpiece to effectively sculpt the part.

The best-known example of this technique is commonly used on the scroll saw's larger cousin, the band saw, to make cabriole legs. Cabriole legs are those delightful S-shaped legs found on Queen Anne furniture and other period pieces. The legs may be smoothed gracefully or embellished with light relief carving on the "knees"—typically a leaf pattern, or heavy sculpted carving at the foot of the leg. The ball-and-claw foot pattern was extremely popular for a while. Antique collectors and aficionados can even tell you when a piece was made and sometimes by whom, just by looking at the foot of a cabriole leg. The type, shape, number of claws, etc., are all clues they can use to help identify the maker.

Cabriole legs are still cut primarily on the band saw because the stock they're made from is typically $2^1/_2$" to 3" square—and this is beyond the cutting capacity of a scroll saw. Folks who make miniatures, however, prefer the scroll saw for shaping tiny cabriole legs. It's a natural choice, since a scroll saw blade leaves such a smooth surface compared to the rough surface commonly produced by the band saw.

Cutting sequence

Three-dimensional shapes are easy to make on the scroll saw using the compound sawing technique. A pattern is applied to two adjoining sides of a blank. Then one side is cut. The waste from the first side is reattached to the workpiece, and the second side is cut to form the 3-D part; see the top photo and the drawing at left.

COMPOUND CUT

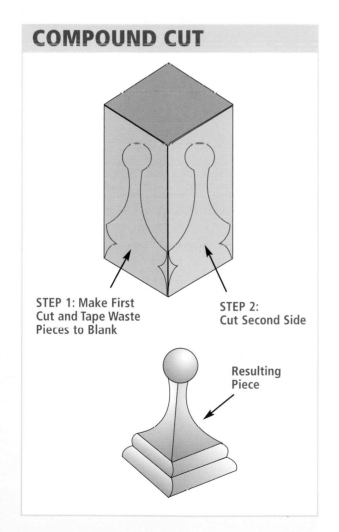

STEP 1: Make First Cut and Tape Waste Pieces to Blank

STEP 2: Cut Second Side

Resulting Piece

Apply pattern to two sides

To make a compound cut on the scroll saw, start by cutting two patterns to fit the blank and then attach them to the blank with spray adhesive or rubber cement, as shown in the top photo. If the part you're making is supposed to be a true 3-D piece, take care to orient the patterns on the adjoining sides so the bottoms align and so they are centered on the blank. If either of these is off, the part will come out lopsided.

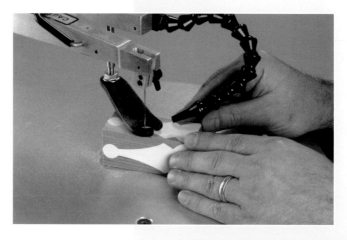

Make first side cuts

Since you'll be removing a lot of wood when you're cutting into a thick blank, it's best to use a blade that has plenty of space between the gullets to help clear the kerf of sawdust. A skip-tooth blade or precision-ground blade works best for this; see page 31. Slow down your feed rate and take your time with these cuts—any mistakes will show up in 3-D. Cut carefully and make sure you save the waste pieces or cutoffs (middle photo).

Make second side cuts

Once you've cut the first side, reattach the waste pieces or cutoffs from the first cut to the blank. Masking tape or duct tape works best for this. Why attach the waste pieces? The second side pattern is likely to be attached to the waste pieces, and you'll need this to make the second cut. What's more, without these pieces, the workpiece won't lie flat on the table. When you've got the waste attached, go ahead and make the cuts on the second side, as shown in the bottom photo. After removing all the waste, you'll be left with your 3-D part.

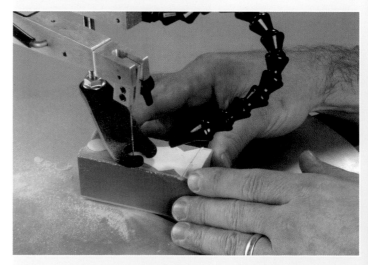

PIERCED COMPOUND CUTS

The opposite of a standard compound cut on the scroll saw is a pierced cut. With a standard compound cut, the cuts are made on the exterior edges of the workpiece to create a sculpted part. On a pierced compound cut, the cuts are made inside the part to create a sculpted interior, as shown in the top photo. Although not often called for, this type of cut can be quite effective in adding visual interest to parts and projects like bud vases and lamp bases. When used in conjunction with the lathe, you can create interesting designs inside turned parts like spindles and holiday ornaments.

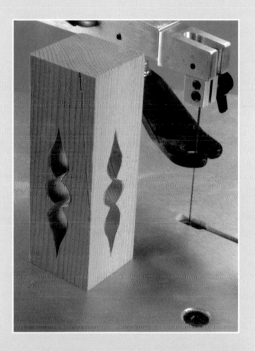

Making the cuts. The technique used for pierced compound sawing is similar to standard compound sawing. A pattern is affixed to or drawn on adjoining sides of the workpiece. Next, one side is cut, and then the adjacent side is cut as shown in the bottom photo. The big difference between the two techniques is that unlike standard compound sawing, you don't need to save and reattach the waste pieces to the blank when making pierced compound cuts. That's because you don't cut into the edges. So, the pattern and the workpiece both stay intact—there are no concerns about the workpiece lying flat on the saw table.

It's important to note that since the two patterns likely won't touch at the edges or perimeter of the workpiece, you'll need to really take your time when attaching these to make sure they're aligned. It's a good idea to draw crosshair reference lines on adjoining faces to make centering the patterns as easy as possible.

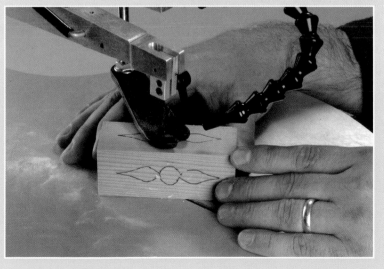

Additionally, unlike with standard compound sawing, you will need to drill access holes in order to make pierced compound cuts. As usual, thicker stock requires a blade that can keep the kerf clear; skip-tooth or precision-ground-tooth blades will work best here (see page 31 for more on these blades).

Fretwork

Webster's dictionary defines fretwork as "decoration consisting of work adorned with frets." And frets are described as "an ornament or ornamental work often in relief." In the land of scrolling, fretwork generally refers to any part that features one or more pierced cuts. In the minds of many, fretwork is simply any fancy, highly detailed scrolled work.

Since fretwork tends to be fragile because of all the pierced cuts, it's important to use the right materials; see the sidebar below. Also, where you drill your access holes to make the pierced cuts and the cutting sequence you choose can determine how successful you are in cutting the piece.

Access holes

There are good spots and bad spots for access holes. A good spot will let you make a clean, pierced cut with no bumps. Bad spots for entry holes make it difficult to start and complete cuts without bumps. The left drawing illustrates good spots for access holes. Note that whenever possible an entry hole is positioned directly in front of a point where two lines intersect. This makes it easy to make the curved cut in both directions. If no possibility for this placement exists, place the hole in the center of the pierced cut, as shown in the left drawing below.

Cutting sequence

The sequence of your pierced cuts is also important. Generally, it's best to cut from the interior out toward the perimeter of the part, as shown in the right drawing below. This way, the inner cuts are supported by the perimeter wood and the likelihood of a break or fracture is lessened.

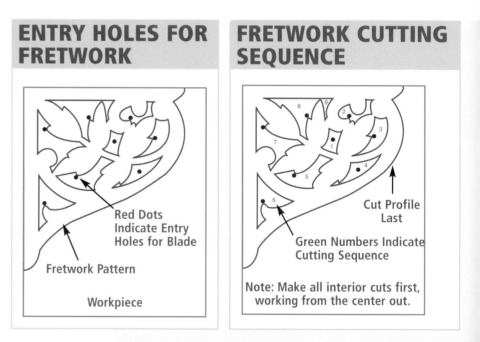

ENTRY HOLES FOR FRETWORK

Red Dots Indicate Entry Holes for Blade

Fretwork Pattern

Workpiece

FRETWORK CUTTING SEQUENCE

Cut Profile Last

Green Numbers Indicate Cutting Sequence

Note: Make all interior cuts first, working from the center out.

MATERIALS FOR FRETWORK

When you combine the thin material that many scrolled projects are made of and the multiple pierced cuts, you can end up with a very fragile part. This is particularly applicable to solid wood. When this is used for a piece of fretwork, the likelihood of a piece breaking off is high. That's because the grain of the wood will be weak at one or more points of the pattern and will easily break off, as shown in the bottom photo. Plywood—particularly premium plywood (page 43)—is a better choice for fretwork: Its cross-ply construction creates a strong, thin material that prevents fractures.

FRETWORK ASSEMBLIES

Because the materials used for fretwork are usually so thin, special joints are required to join pieces of fretwork together. Two of the more common are the tab and slot and the locking tab and slot joints, as illustrated in the top drawing.

The tab and slot is sort of a mortise-and-tenon joint, but it lacks the mechanical strength this classic joint normally offers; the slot is the mortise and the tab is the tenon. The thin materials do not provide a lot of glue surface, so you can't rely on this joint to hold up under any pressure.

Although the locking tab and slot joint doesn't offer much more in terms of glue surface, it does offer better mechanical strength, as the tab passes completely through the slot and "locks" the part in place. This joint is commonly used without glue so that the parts can be knocked down and disassembled for storage.

TAB & SLOT AND LOCKING TABS FOR FRETWORK

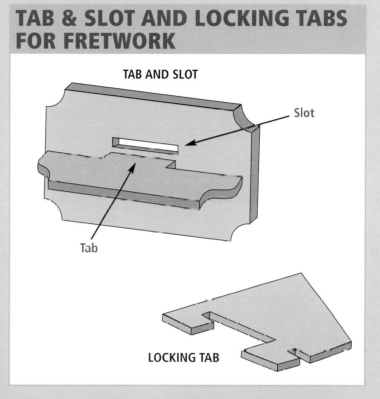

TAB AND SLOT

Slot

Tab

LOCKING TAB

Step 1: Insert locking tab in slot until the back of the tabbed piece butts up against the face of the slotted piece.

Step 2: Slide the tabbed piece over until it butts up against the inside edge of the slot.

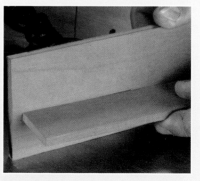

Step 3: When the locked tab piece is slid over completely, it should totally conceal the slot. To disassemble, just reverse the process.

Inlay Work

A scroll saw excels at inlay work. That's because it can cut super-tight curves and will gently cut stock as thin as veneer. Although most inlay work is in fact done with veneer, you can use thicker stock if you like. Additionally, thicker stock provides the opportunity to sculpt the inlay (for more on sculpted inlays, see page 96). There are two basic methods to cutting inlay: straight and bevel-sawn. With either method, you can use a stack-cutting technique that will ensure that the pieces fit together nicely.

Straight-cut method

The straight-cut method of inlay is the simplest, since there are no angles to worry about. The disadvantage to this method is that the gap left by the saw blade—the kerf—is often visible, especially where light and dark parts meet.

To make an inlay using the straight-cut method, start by cutting your veneer to size. You'll need as many sheets as the different colors your project plan requires. For the inlay we're making here, we used three veneers: maple, cherry, and walnut. Stack these veneers together and tape them to a thin piece of plywood ($1/8$") or cardboard (top photo). This backer board will not only help support the fragile veneer, but it will also help prevent tear-out by backing up the cuts.

Next, install a fine blade in the saw—a number 9 works well—and if possible, replace your standard table insert with a zero-clearance insert (for more on these, see page 77). If you are making pierced cuts (as we are here), drill or punch access holes in the veneer sandwich. Now you can cut out the inlays. As you work, keep your fingers as safely close to the blade as possible to prevent the veneer from fracturing. Take your time here: Keep pressing down on the veneer sandwich at all times to keep the blade from lifting it off the saw table, as shown in the middle photo. As you near the end of a cut, apply pressure to both the veneer sandwich and any parts that may

be cut free. Stop the saw and remove any freed parts as they are separated from the veneer sandwich.

When you're done cutting, carefully remove the tape. Now you can mix and match the inlays with the borders as you please; see the bottom photo.

To use an inlay and its matching border, position the inlay in the border and secure it with veneer tape—this will be the top of the inlay. Then glue the taped veneer/border to your project stock. When the glue is dry, moisten the tape and scrape it off with a cabinet scraper.

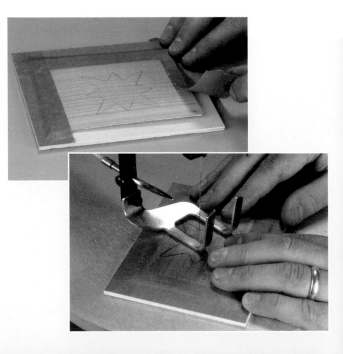

Bevel-sawn method

The bevel-sawn method of cutting inlays is almost identical to the straight-sawn method. The only difference is that the saw table is tilted a few degrees, as shown in the top photo. The angled cut helps reduce the gap created by the saw kerf and produces a tighter inlay. To bevel-saw an inlay, stack the veneers just as you would with straight-sawn. Use the same cutting technique, but first tilt the table to about 3 or 4 degrees. When you're done and you mix and match the inlays with the borders, you'll find that they fit together tighter, with less gap showing.

Solid-wood inlays

If you don't like the idea of working with such fragile stock as veneer, you can still make inlays—just use thicker stock. Eighth-inch stock like that shown in the middle photo works well for this. Because they're thicker, you can temporarily attach the pieces

together with double-faced tape as shown. This creates an even thicker blank that's much less prone to fracturing than veneer. Cut this blank as you would any other piece of wood on the scroll saw; you don't need to keep your fingers as close to the blade, since the layers are joined together.

You will still need to be careful, though, when it's time to separate the pieces (bottom photo). Drizzling a little lacquer thinner between the layers will help dissolve the adhesive so you can pull the parts apart without fear of damaging them.

SCULPTED INLAYS

If you want to add some depth to your inlay work and give it a 3-D look, consider using thicker stock and then shaping the edges. This is very similar to intarsia, as described on pages 98–100.

Stack and cut. To make a sculpted inlay, begin by temporarily attaching the inlay stock to the border stock with double-faced tape. Then attach the pattern to the inlay stock and cut out the inlay as shown in the top photo. No special cutting techniques are required here; this is basic scrolling.

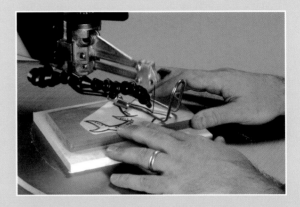

Shape the inlay. When you've completed the cut, separate the pieces and set the border layer aside. Now you can shape the edges—and even the face—of the inlay as desired. This can be done with a file (as shown in the middle photo), with carving tools, or with sandpaper. It's a good idea to periodically place the inlay in the border to see how it looks. Continue shaping until the desired effect is achieved.

Attach the inlay. There are a couple of ways you can attach the inlay. The first method is to fasten the inlay to the border with glue. Hot-melt glue works well for this, as it bridges gaps and sets up quickly. Apply a bead around the perimeter of the inlay to lock it in place as shown in the bottom photo. Alternatively, you can glue the inlay and the border to a thin base layer. This method is the most secure because the entire bottom of the inlay is glued to the base instead of just around the perimeter with the hot-melt glue.

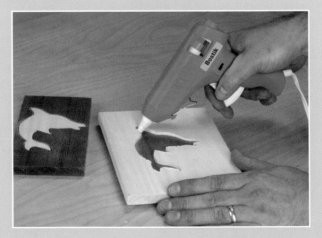

Cutting with Spiral Blades

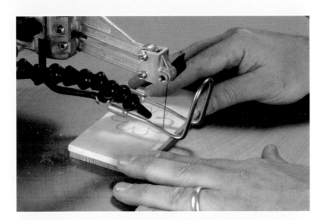

Because you can cut in any direction with a spiral blade, you'd think these would be easy to use—and they are. But they take some getting used to. Unlike a standard blade, where the teeth point in only one direction, a spiral blade is twisted so that the teeth provide 360-degree cutting action.

Saw in any direction

The 360-degree cutting action means you can move the workpiece in any direction without spinning or turning the workpiece. This is the part that takes some getting used to. Scrollers learn from day one that blades cut in only one direction, so they have to always present the workpiece to the blade properly to make the cut.

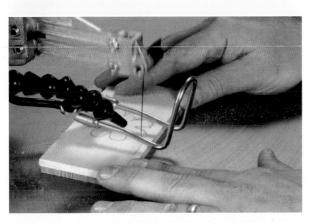

With a spiral blade you can go back and forth (top photo) and side to side (middle photo) without changing the orientation of the workpiece to the blade. For example, you can cut a "W" shape in a workpiece using a spiral blade with the front edge of the workpiece parallel to the front of the saw table the entire time.

Finished cut is rough

If you can cut in any direction at any time with a spiral blade, why would you use any other blade? Because spiral blades have some drawbacks. First,

because the teeth are twisted and not aligned, when you make a cut, some of the teeth will always be cutting against the grain and have a tendency to tear-out or splinter the surface. So you'll typically end up with a rougher cut with a spiral blade, as shown in the bottom photo. Second, the wrap-around teeth also create a much wider kerf than a standard blade does. This is less of a problem for general scrolling, but significant when cutting inlays, intarsia, or marquetry.

Intarsia and Segmentation

Intarsia and segmentation are similar techniques that have been gaining popularity with scrollers for years. In both methods, wood is cut into smaller parts, shaped, and then glued back together. With intarsia, different species of wood are often used to create different textures and colors, as shown in the top photo. The parts of a segmentation project, on the other hand, are typically cut from a single piece of wood, as shown in the middle photo.

Because intarsia uses different woods, you'll often need multiple patterns, whereas with segmentation, you'll need only one. The shaping you do to the parts can be as simple as a uniform roundover, like the parts of the heart in the middle photo, or as complex as the heavily shaped fruit and leaves in the top photo.

Cutting out the parts

For the most part, scrolling the parts for an intarsia or segmentation project requires no special techniques. The only thing to be careful of is small parts. You'll want to use one or more of the cutting techniques described on page 76 when dealing with small parts. Also, it's a good idea to number the parts before you cut them out, and set aside a "master" pattern with matching numbers. This lets you assemble the parts together later without getting confused. Tip: If you number the parts of the pattern, transfer these numbers to the bottom of the parts once they have been cut out. This way, when you remove the pattern for shaping the top, you'll still know which part you're working on and where it goes.

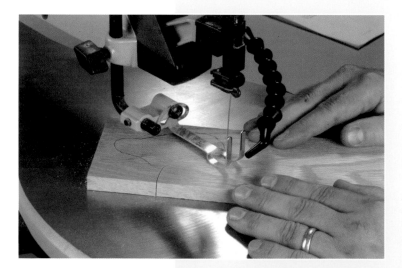

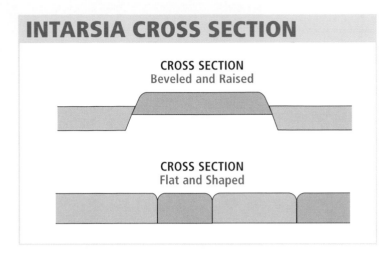

INTARSIA CROSS SECTION

CROSS SECTION
Beveled and Raised

CROSS SECTION
Flat and Shaped

Straight versus bevel-sawn

To achieve a 3-D effect, the individual parts of an intarsia or segmentation project are often of varying heights (thickness). You can use different-thickness stock, but in some cases this isn't possible or feasible—either the wood is too expensive or you just can't find a source. In cases like this, consider bevel-sawing adjoining parts, as shown in the top drawing. Sawing at an angle will allow you to push up a "thicker" piece to create a 3-D effect. The only consideration here is that the beveled piece will need to be secured to the adjoining pieces instead of directly to the background or foundation piece.

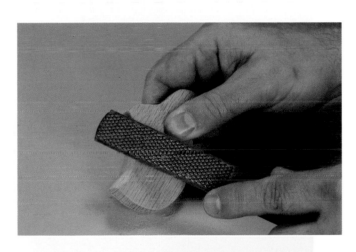

Shaping by hand

Once all the parts are cut out, you can begin shaping them. A four-in-hand rasp like the one shown in the middle photo works fine for this. Yes, this does require some elbow grease, but slowly filing a profile prevents you from taking off more than you want (which is easy to do with power tools). The guideline to remember is, start with the thinnest pieces first and shape them. Then butt the thicker adjoining pieces up against these and mark where they meet to make it easier to contour the thicker pieces.

Shaping with a sanding drum

A sanding drum fitted in a portable drill (as shown in the bottom photo) or in a drill press makes quick work of shaping parts. Another excellent sanding tool is an air-filled drum for the lathe. These drums have an air valve that lets you vary the pressure inside so you can create a soft and flexible or a hard sanding surface, and anything in between. Two other useful sanding accessories are mop and flap wheels. Both of these use strips of sandpaper mounted to a hub that fits in your portable drill or drill press. Both excel at sanding contours and can be bought through most mail-order woodworking suppliers.

Shaping with a router

The quickest way to profile edges for intarsia and segmentation projects is with a router fitted with a round-over bit, as shown in the top photo. Even small parts can be safely profiled, as long as you use a routing mat to keep the part from shifting during routing. The drawback to routing is that it does leave a uniform edge. This is fine for many segmentation projects, but won't provide the sculpted look you're after in intarsia. Nevertheless, a router is an excellent tool to remove the bulk of the material along an edge prior to sculpting by hand or using some type of sander.

Gluing up the parts

There are two basic methods for gluing up intarsia and segmentation projects. The first method is to cut a background from solid wood or plywood and glue the parts directly to this, as shown in the middle photo. This background remains visible as sort of a frame for the project. The other method is to cut a thin plywood back that's about 1/4" smaller around the perimeter of the project and glue the parts to this. This creates a frameless or floating project, where the background is hidden.

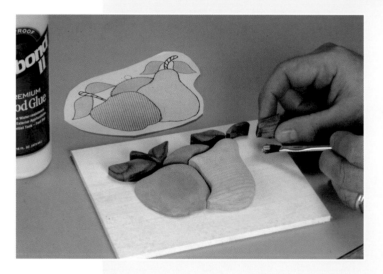

STAINING OR DYEING PARTS

Not everyone has a scrap bin filled with exotic woods or can afford the varying species needed to create interesting and colorful intarsia and segmentation projects. An inexpensive alternative to using different woods for a project is to cut them all from a single board and then stain or dye the parts to achieve the desired look. Dyes tend to let the grain show through (bottom photo), while many stains obscure the grain. What you use depends on the look you're after.

Overlays

An overlay is the opposite of an inlay; instead of fitting into a recess cut into the project or background, an overlay rests on top. This is really an extension of intarsia (pages 98–100), except instead of being a stand-alone project, overlay is primarily used as decoration. Sadly, this is an underused technique: An overlay can add just the right touch to a project to raise it from ordinary to distinctive. An example of this is the decoration added to the ready-made shelf shown in the top photo. An excellent source for inlay patterns is stained-glass patterns. These can be used with no modification, as the parts are glued directly to the background.

Cut out parts

In most cases, overlays are cut from fairly thin stock, $\frac{1}{4}$" or less. The $\frac{1}{8}$" stock chosen for the shelf can be cut as is (middle photo); but if your pattern calls for parts with delicate or thin shapes, you'll be better off temporarily attaching the stock to a thin plywood backer board before cutting. This will help prevent the fine details of the thin stock from fracturing. A fine double-tooth or crown-tooth blade will do a nice job of cutting smooth edges in thin stock.

Glue to background

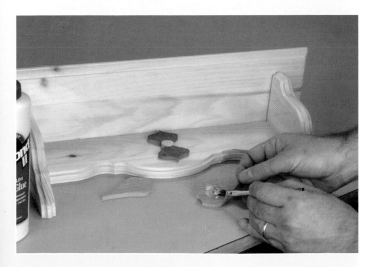

Once the parts are cut to size, you can attach them to the background. Depending on the thickness of the overlay and the design, you may or may not want to shape or sculpt the edges before gluing them in place. For thin stock, this can be accomplished quickly by hand with sandpaper or with a sanding drum fitted in a portable drill or drill press. It's a good idea to draw a set of light crosshair reference lines on the background as an aid to positioning the overlay pieces. Take care to keep the glue a good $\frac{1}{4}$" in from the edges of the pieces to prevent glue from squeezing out. If the parts are all the same thickness, you can clamp them in place by simply setting a weight on top. For varying-thickness parts, a bag of sand works well, as it will shape itself to fit the parts.

Coping with the Scroll Saw

When it comes to joinery, the scroll saw is the perfect tool for cutting coped joints. Coped joints are used extensively by savvy trim carpenters and woodworkers who want moldings to intersect at inside corners without the gaps normally associated with miter joints. There are two halves to a coped joint; see the drawing below right. On one half, the molding profile is left intact and simply butted into the corner of a wall or cabinet. The second half is the part that's coped to fit the profile of the molding butted into the corner.

When done properly, a coped part will butt cleanly up against the molding profile with no gaps, as shown in the top photo. Not only will this joint fit nicely when completed, but it will also stay that way: There's less exposed end grain than with a miter joint, which will expand and contract as the seasons change. Miter joints are notorious for opening and closing as the humidity changes, producing a varying-width gap throughout the year.

COPED JOINT

Expose the cope

To make a coped joint, start by installing one molding piece so it butts into the corner. The next step is to expose the cope on the molding to be coped. This can be done on a number of power saws, such as the table saw shown in the bottom photo. The idea here is to cut the end as if you were doing an inside miter. The miter cut will expose the wood that needs to be removed to fit against the matching profile of the first piece.

Remove the waste

Once you've exposed the cope, you can remove the waste. Here's where the scroll saw shines. Normally, the waste is removed with a coping saw, but this is hard to do with any precision. However, a scroll saw fitted with a fine blade will make quick work of this since it's much easier to control the workpiece, as shown in the top photo. It's best to make a series of relief cuts first where the molding profile changes direction. Then go back and cut out the waste, taking care not to cut into the face of the molding.

Test the fit

After you've removed the exposed cope, try fitting the coped piece against a scrap of the molding as shown in the middle photo. Note any areas where there are gaps, and mark these with a pencil. If there are large gaps, go back to the scroll saw and remove the bulk of the waste. If the gaps are small, you can fine-tune the joint as described below.

Fine-tune the fit

When small gaps occur between the coped piece and the molding, it's usually easiest to fine-tune the coped profile to fit better. A small round file will generally make quick work of this, as shown in the bottom photo. Be sure to angle the file slightly back toward the back of the molding to keep from filing into the exposed profile. Alternatively, a dowel or screw-driver wrapped with sandpaper can quickly remove waste from curved areas. Test the fit frequently and continue fine-tuning until the coped part fits perfectly against the molding profile.

Cutting Dovetail Joints

The dovetail joint gets its name from the tail half of the joint, which resembles the shape of a dove's tail; see the drawing at right. The other half of the joint is the pins, which fit into the openings between the tails, as shown in the drawing. Many wood-workers view the dovetail joint as the ultimate way to join wood. The dovetail joint is both attractive and incredibly strong; see the top photo.

Cutting precise dovetails by hand requires a steady hand, a keen eye, and razor-sharp tools—not to mention considerable practice. Cutting precise dovetails with a scroll saw is much easier, since most of the waste is removed by the saw. This leaves only a little bit of chisel work to clean up the joints and fine-tune the fit.

Lay out the joint
A dovetail gauge like the one shown in the bottom photo is a quick way to lay out the parts of a dovetail joint. Most gauges offer the two most common angles for dovetails: a 1:8 slope for hardwoods and a 1:6 slope for softwoods.

To use a dovetail marker, first use a marking gauge to set the depth of the tails to match the thickness of the wood. Then carefully lay out the tail spacing. Position the dovetail marker so that it aligns with one of the marks and so the slope is in the correct direction. Then mark the side of the tail as shown. Flip the gauge over and mark the opposite side. Continue like this until all the tails have been marked. (Note: We recommend cutting the tails first and then using these to lay out the pins.)

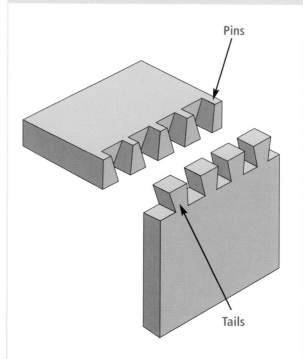

DOVETAIL ANATOMY

Pins

Tails

Cut the tails

Once you've laid out the pins on the ends of your project parts, you can cut them out with the scroll saw as shown in the top photo. Because the scroll saw can handle tight-radius curves, you can make the cut in a single pass by making a pair of on-the-spot turns at the bottom of each tail (taking care to stay on the waste side of the marked lines). When you've cut all the tails, go back with a chisel and remove any waste up to the lines and sharpen the corners at the bottom of the tails where the sides meet the bottom, as shown in the inset photo.

Cut the pins

To mark the pins, position the appropriate tail piece on the end of the pin piece and mark the pins (see the top photo on page 130 for an example of this). Then tilt the saw table to the desired slope and cut one side of each of the pins, as shown in the middle photo. Tilt the saw table in the opposite direction and cut the other side of the pins; see the middle inset photo. Note: If your table tilts in only one direction, make an angled sled to cut the sides opposite your first cuts.

Remove the waste

When you've made all the side cuts for the pins, remove the waste between the pins with a chisel, as shown in the bottom photo. Make sure to clamp the workpiece firmly in place to a backer board to prevent damage to your workbench or work surface. To prevent chip-out and create a more accurate pin, chisel only about halfway through the waste, levering out the waste as you go. Then flip the workpiece over and remove the remaining waste. Test the fit and fine-tune as necessary.

Slip Joint

In addition to the slot and tab and the locking tab and slot joints described on page 93, the slip joint is another way to join together thin or delicate scrolled parts. The slip joint is just a pair of opposing slots cut in the pieces to be joined; see the top drawing. Although this joint doesn't offer a lot of glue surface, the surfaces are edge grain to face grain, which makes a fairly strong glue joint.

see the top drawing

Cut the slots

The secret to cutting a strong slip joint is to lay out the slots accurately and cut them a bit on the fat side, as shown in the middle photo. This way you can go back with a chisel and pare the slots to width to create a friction fit. Alternatively, you can tune the slots with a small mill file or a sanding stick, as described on page 75.

Slip the parts together

Whichever method you use to tune the slots, stop frequently and test the fit. What you want are parts that slide together with a little friction and will stay in place once released. When you like the fit, you can join these parts together permanently with glue. Apply a thin coat into the slot on one piece and slip the parts together. If you apply glue to both slots, you'll likely get squeeze-out, which can be a real challenge to remove on delicate parts.

SLIP JOINT

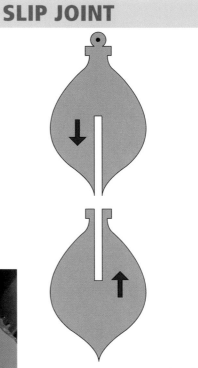

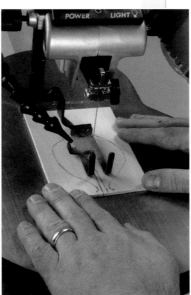

Marquetry

Marquetry is basically painting with wood. It really is an art form. Accomplished marquetry pros can create images that are highly detailed and amazingly lifelike. These can be simple decorations inlaid into solid-wood projects, or ornate portraits, or pictures that stand alone as art. Although there are special saws designed just for making the delicate cuts necessary for marquetry, many scrollers have had excellent results with a standard scroll saw.

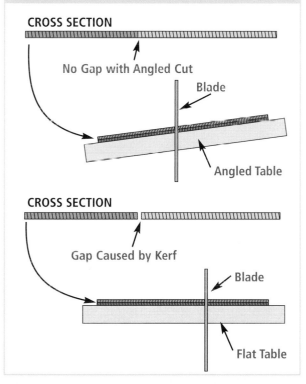

STACKED MARQUETRY CUTS

CROSS SECTION

No Gap with Angled Cut

Blade

Angled Table

CROSS SECTION

Gap Caused by Kerf

Blade

Flat Table

Sandwich the veneers

Marquetry involves cutting individual pieces of veneer to fit together to form a larger image. In many cases, veneers are stacked up and cut at the same time to create parts that can be mixed and matched to fit perfectly together. Start by selecting the veneers you want as a color palette. Then stack them together with the pattern you'll be working with on top. Attach them to a thin plywood or cardboard backer with masking tape, as shown in the top photo.

Making stacked cuts

You can, of course, cut the veneer pieces out separately from single sheets of veneer, but it takes a keen eye and a steady hand to cut profiles to match—something that's guaranteed when you stack-cut veneers. Stack-cutting can be done straight or at an angle; see the drawing at left. When you angle the saw table slightly, you'll create parts that will fit together seamlessly—something that doesn't happen when you straight-saw the parts, as there will always be a gap formed by the saw kerf.

STARTER HOLES

For marquetry parts to fit together perfectly, there can't be any access holes—even for the narrow blades you'll be using (see page 108). Of course, you'll still need to make holes for the blade to pass through the veneer sandwich, but you can't drill them because the hole would be large and obvious. The solution is to "punch" a tiny hole with a pin or brad fitted into the end of a dowel, as shown in the bottom photo. To keep this hole as small as possible, consider modifying the blade as described on page 157.

Choosing a blade

The blade you choose to cut the veneer will have a huge impact on how successful you are at cutting the pieces to size without damage. In terms of size, a 3/0 or 2/0 blade will work best. Depending on the type of blade, these sizes will have between 20 and 35 teeth per inch. Skip-tooth, reverse-tooth, and crown-tooth blades are your best bet here; see pages 31, 32, and 34, respectively, for more on these blade types. If you do decide to use a reverse-tooth blade, make sure to modify the blade as necessary to prevent splintering, as described on page 71.

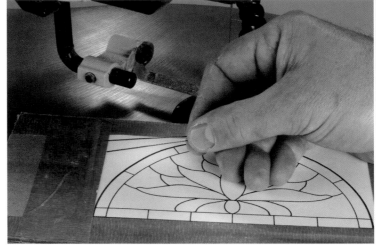

Preventing damage

Because veneer is so fragile, anything you can do to help support it when cutting lessens the likelihood of the veneer fracturing or splitting. A simple way to fully support the veneer is to replace your standard table insert with a zero-clearance insert, as shown in the middle photo. If you don't have one of these, you can still support the veneer by adding a zero-clearance top to the table, as described on page 77.

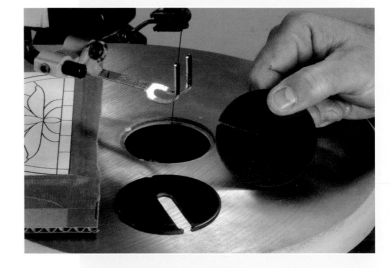

Bevel-sawing

When you've mounted the desired blade in the lower arm mounting clamps and have punched your veneer sandwich as needed to make any pierced cuts, you can thread the blade through the sandwich. This can be quite tricky since the access hole is so small; underlighting can help. The Olson Fretlite as described on page 39 is designed just for this job, or you can place a small desk lamp or trouble light nearby to serve the same purpose. Once you've clamped the top of the blade in place and have tensioned the blade properly, you can begin cutting. If desired, angle the table 3 or 4 degrees as shown in the bottom photo, turn on the saw, and cut, taking care to support the veneer as close to the blade as possible while still maintaining a safe distance.

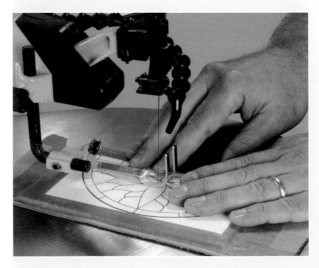

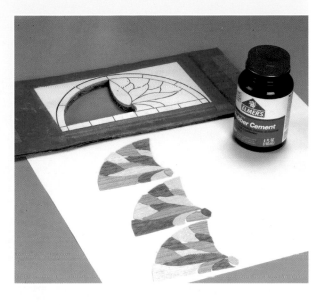

Gluing up

Once you've cut all the parts to size, set them out in the original pattern so that you can glue them up, as shown in the top photo. There are a couple of ways to do this. One is to begin by bonding the parts temporarily to a copy of the pattern; this way you know all the parts are in the right place. Then use rubber cement to attach a layer of kraft paper to the veneer. Carefully flip the veneer over and remove the pattern. Now you can attach this to your foundation wood—typically high-quality plywood. Use yellow glue for this and set another piece of plywood on top of the veneer, followed by weights (bricks work well for this: You can position them to weigh down the entire surface). Allow the glue to dry overnight and remove the weights and plywood. Dampen the kraft paper with water and carefully peel it off. Sand the veneered surface smooth, and fill any gaps with a mixture of glue and matching sawdust.

SHADING

If you take a close look at a piece of marquetry done by a professional, you'll usually see sections of parts that seem to be shaded to make them appear more three-dimensional. And they are shaded—but not with paint, stain, or ink. Instead, the parts are shaded with heat—they are actually scorched to create shadows as shown in the photos at right. You don't have to be a pro to try this. All you need is a metal bowl and some clean, dry play sand. Fill the bowl about two-thirds full and set it on a heat source—an old camp stove or single burner electric heater works great for this. Adjust the burner for mid-high heat, and let the sand heat up for about a half-hour.

To shade a part, grab it with a pair of tweezers and place the edge you want to shade in the heated sand. Hold it there for a moment and check to see how it looks; see the top right photo. The amount of shading and how dark it is will depend on how much of the part contacts the sand and how long you hold it in the sand.

Yes, there is skill involved here, but with some practice, it's not that difficult to learn. Before you try shading any project parts, take the time to practice first—and make sure to try different species. You'll quickly learn that different woods scorch quicker than others. You might want to make some notes or keep some scraps that you've shaded, noting how long you held each in place. This way you won't have to experiment the next time you want to shade a part.

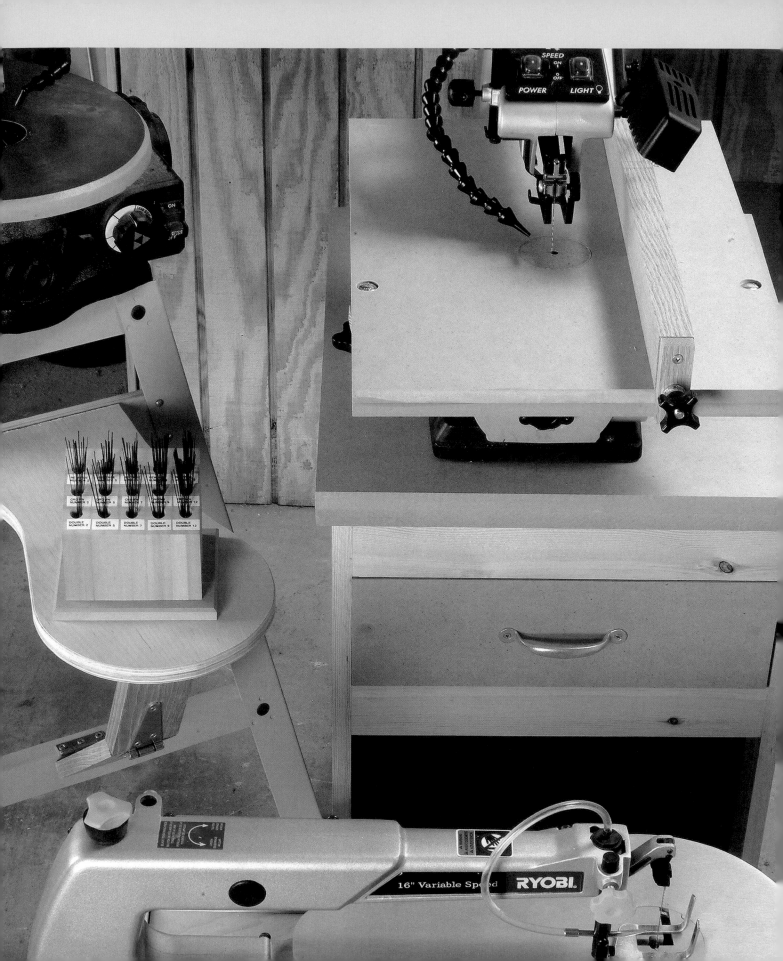

5 Shop-Made Jigs and Fixtures

What exactly is a jig? According to the dictionary, it's "a device used to maintain mechanically the correct positional relationship between a piece of work and the tool." And a fixture? That's "a device for supporting work during machining." To both definitions, let's add "or a device that makes a tool easier, safer, or more comfortable to use." That's what most of the jigs and fixtures designed for scroll saws do.

The jigs and fixtures designed for scroll saws don't necessarily add precision the way they can with other machines—precision in scrolling is mainly a by-product of the scroller's skill and patience. But it's difficult to acquire skill and have patience if the machine you're using is uncomfortable. None of the projects in this chapter will add precision to your scroll saw. What they will do is make it easier and safer to use your saw, while helping you relax and be comfortable so that you can enjoy your time scrolling.

The saw stand and sand-filled base shown here reduce vibration and position a saw at the correct height. The knock-down seat offers a convenient place to sit and enjoy your scrolling. A saw table with fence extends the life of your blades while allowing you to rip stock to width on the scroll saw.

Auxiliary Table with Fence

An auxiliary table for a scroll saw is a good idea for a couple of reasons. For starters, it increases the size of the top to provide a more stable platform for scrolling. Second, a square table lets you add a fence for making precise rips as shown in the top photo. Third, an auxiliary table extends the life of your blades. That's because the stroke of a blade is quite short—typically $3/4$". The table raises the workpiece anywhere from $1/2$" to $3/4$" (however thick you make the auxiliary top), which means that a "fresh" part of the blade is exposed for the cut. To make blade-changing easier, the auxiliary table shown here has a removable insert much like the insert on your saw's table top.

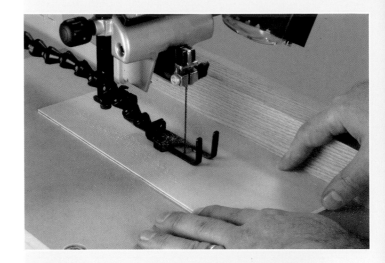

Glue on edging

To make the auxiliary table, start by determining the measurements for the top and edging; see the exploded view and materials list on the opposite page. For the table to fit your saw, measure the width and length of your saw's top and add 3" to both dimensions to provide clearance for the edging. Note: The dimensions described here are just suggestions; you can make the table as large as you'd like. Cut the table and edging to size and glue the edging around the perimeter of the top as shown in the middle photo.

Drill insert hole in top

Although you can omit the table insert by simply drilling a hole in the top, the insert will make changing and threading blades a lot easier. To locate the hole's position, place the table on your saw top and mark up through the saw's insert opening. We used a 2" hole saw to drill the hole, as shown in the bottom photo.

Rout rabbet for insert

For the insert to fit flush with the top of the table, rout a $1/4$"-deep rabbet around the perimeter of the hole you just drilled, as shown in the top photo. If you use a $1/4$"-wide rabbetting bit, this will create a $2^1/2$"-diameter opening for the insert. We used an adjustable circle cutter to make the insert. The pilot hole of the circle cutter leaves a $1/4$" hole in the center of the insert for the blade to pass through.

EXPLODED VIEW

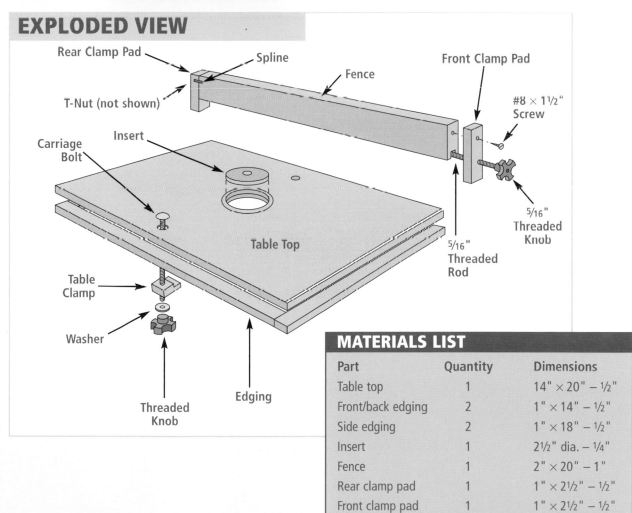

Rear Clamp Pad
Spline
Fence
Front Clamp Pad
T-Nut (not shown)
#8 × 1½" Screw
Carriage Bolt
Insert
$5/16$" Threaded Knob
Table Top
$5/16$" Threaded Rod
Table Clamp
Washer
Threaded Knob
Edging

MATERIALS LIST

Part	Quantity	Dimensions
Table top	1	14" × 20" − ½"
Front/back edging	2	1" × 14" − ½"
Side edging	2	1" × 18" − ½"
Insert	1	2½" dia. − ¼"
Fence	1	2" × 20" − 1"
Rear clamp pad	1	1" × 2½" − ½"
Front clamp pad	1	1" × 2½" − ½"
Spline	1	½" × 1" − ⅛"
Table clamps	2	1" × 1½" − 1"

Make the table clamps

The auxiliary table attaches to your saw's top with a pair of table clamps. These are nothing more than two small blocks that are rabbetted to fit over the edge of your saw table; see the clamp detail in the drawing below. To make the clamps safely, first cut the rabbet on an oversized blank. Then trim the blanks to width and length. Drill holes in the clamps for carriage bolts. Next, locate the best position for the clamps and drill counterbored holes in the sides of the table for the carriage bolts to pass through, as shown in the top photo.

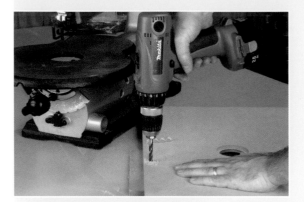

Attach clamps to table

Place the auxiliary top on your saw and insert a carriage bolt in each hole in the top. Slip a table clamp over each bolt, and thread on a washer and a plastic threaded knob or wing nut, as shown in the middle photo. What you're looking for here is a slight gap between the top of the table clamp and the underside of the auxiliary table top, as illustrated in the clamp detail in the drawing below. Trim the clamp or shim as necessary to create a gap to let the clamp pinch the saw table between the bottom of the clamp and the auxiliary table.

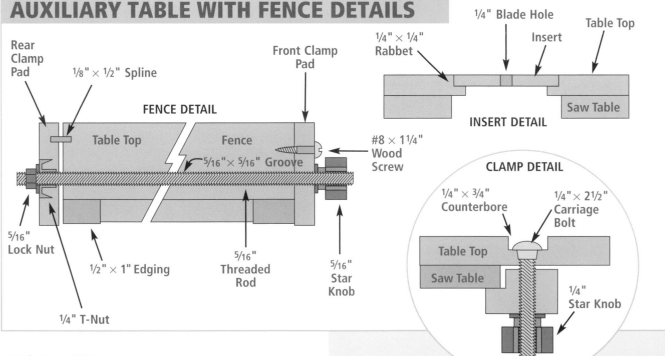

AUXILIARY TABLE WITH FENCE DETAILS

Rear Clamp Pad

$1/8" \times 1/2"$ Spline

Front Clamp Pad

FENCE DETAIL

Table Top

Fence

$5/16" \times 5/16"$ Groove

#8 × 1 1/4" Wood Screw

$5/16"$ Lock Nut

$1/4"$ T-Nut

$1/2" \times 1"$ Edging

$5/16"$ Threaded Rod

$5/16"$ Star Knob

1/4" Blade Hole

$1/4" \times 1/4"$ Rabbet

Insert

Table Top

Saw Table

INSERT DETAIL

CLAMP DETAIL

$1/4" \times 3/4"$ Counterbore

$1/4" \times 2 1/2"$ Carriage Bolt

Table Top

Saw Table

$1/4"$ Star Knob

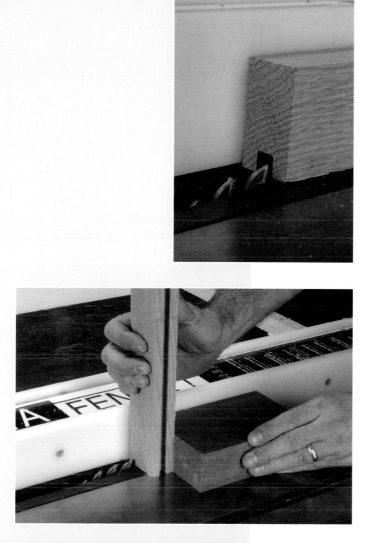

Cut groove in fence

The table fence consists of a fence body and two clamp pads that are pulled together via a threaded rod that is housed in a groove in the fence body; see the fence detail in the drawing on the opposite page. The rod threads into a T-nut on the rear clamp pad and is pulled tight when a threaded knob that attaches to the other end of the rod is turned. To make the fence, start by cutting it to length to match the length of your auxiliary table, less $1/8$". This $1/8$" provides the clearance needed to pinch the top between the clamp pads. Next, cut a centered groove along the length of the fence to accept the threaded rod as shown in the top photo.

Cut kerfs for rear clamp pad

The rear clamp pad is secured to the fence by way of a spline. This spline lets the clamp pad pivot to apply clamping pressure. The spline fits in kerfs cut in the end of the fence body and the top inside face of the rear clamp pad. Adjust the rip fence on your saw to cut the kerf $3/8$" down from the top edge, and use a backer board to make a safe cut as shown in the middle photo. Without moving the fence, use the same set-up to kerf the rear clamp pad.

Install T-nut in rear clamp pad

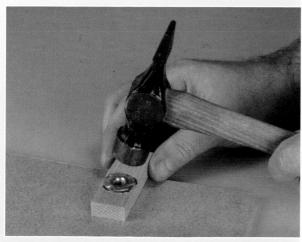

The next step is to install the T-nut in the back face of the rear clamp pad. To locate the hole for this, place the rear clamp pad onto the end of the fence body, taking care to align the kerfs for the spline. Then mark the location of the groove in the bottom of the fence body on the inside face of the rear clamp pad. Drill a hole centered on the marked groove to accept the shank of the T-nut. Finally, install the T-nut by tapping it in place with a hammer as shown in the bottom photo.

Drill holes in front clamp pad

The front clamp pad attaches to the fence by way of a woodscrew near the top of the pad; the threaded rod passes through the pad beneath the woodscrew. To locate the hole for the rod, place the front clamp pad onto the end of the fence body, taking care to align the top of the pad with the top of the fence. Then mark the location of the groove in the bottom of the fence body on the inside face of the front clamp pad. Drill a hole centered on the marked groove slightly larger than the diameter of the threaded rod, as shown in the top photo.

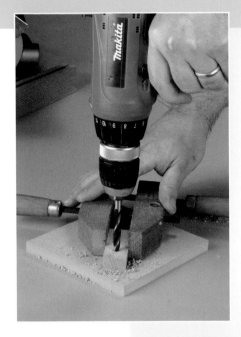

Attach front clamp pad

Now you can attach the front clamp pad to the fence body. Place the clamp pad on the fence body so its top is aligned with the top of the fence. Insert an awl through the top hole into the clamp pad to mark the hole location in the end of the fence body. Remove the clamp pad and drill a pilot hole to accept the woodscrew. Reposition the clamp pad and secure it to the fence with a #8 × 1 1/4" woodscrew, as shown in the middle photo.

Install threaded rod

To determine the length of the threaded rod, temporarily slip it into the groove in the bottom of the fence body as shown in the bottom photo. Slip one end of the rod through the hole in the front clamp pad and slide it down until it contacts the T-nut in the rear clamp pad. Thread the rod into the T-nut as shown in the inset photo. On the end that's sticking out of the front clamp pad, measure out 1" from the front clamp and mark the rod. Remove the rod and cut it to length; file the ends smooth.

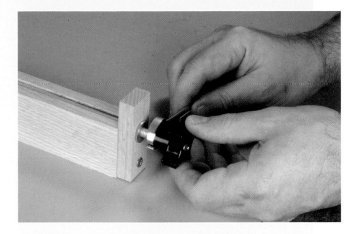

Add the fence knob

With the rod cut to length, all that's left is to install it in the fence and add the front knob. Slip the rod in place and thread it into the T-nut in the rear clamp pad. Then thread on a jam nut and the threaded knob on the rod where it passes through the front clamp pad. Use a wrench to tighten the jam nut onto the knob to keep it from spinning, as shown in the top photo.

USING THE TABLE

The auxiliary table is simple to attach and use. To attach it to your saw, start by removing the saw blade and then lift out the saw table's insert. Removing this insert will make it easier both to change blades with the auxiliary top in place and to thread blades through a workpiece to make a pierced cut.

Attach the table. Position the auxiliary table on your saw top so its insert opening is positioned over the insert opening in the saw top. Rotate the table clamps so the rabbetted edge engages the edge of the saw top. Tighten the knobs below the clamps as needed to lock it firmly in place.

Adjust the fence. You can use the auxiliary table with or without the fence. To use the fence, loosen the fence knob and fit the fence over the table so the front and rear clamp pads engage the front and rear edges of the auxiliary table. Use a tape measure or a rule to measure between the side of the blade and the fence. Then slide the fence as needed to position it for the desired cut, and tighten the fence knob to lock the fence in place.

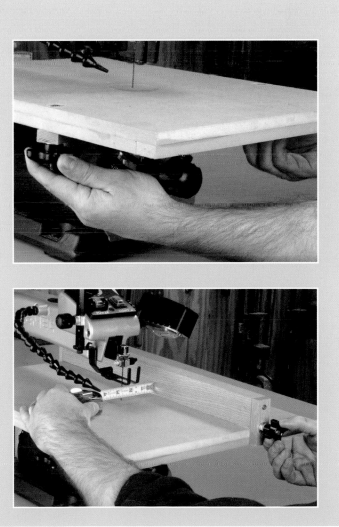

Scroll Saw Blade Holder

One of the challenges of scrolling is keeping track of all the blades you'll probably own. It's darn near impossible for most folks to tell the difference between a 3/0 blade and 2/0 blade. That's why it's so important to use some kind of blade storage that will separate and identify the different types and sizes of blades. The blade holder in the top photo does this, plus its angled top puts the blades at your fingertips. What's unique about this blade holder is that no special hardware is required—no tubes or plastic bottles. Instead, matching sets of coves are routed in the sides of the holder and then glued together to form holes to hold the blades; see the exploded view and materials list on the opposite page.

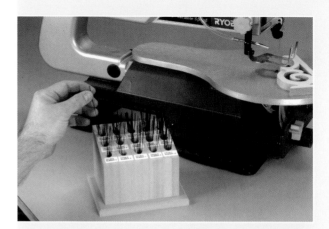

Rout coves in the sides

To make the blade holder shown here, start by cutting the holder side pieces to size from 1/2" medium-density fiberboard (MDF). We used MDF since there's no grain direction to worry about and since it routs smoothly, but you could use just about any material. The coves are routed using a 1/2" core-box bit fitted into a table-mounted router, as shown in the middle photo. Adjust the router table fence to locate the coves as illustrated in the cove detail in the drawing on the opposite page. Rout coves in all the pieces before adjusting the fence for the next cut.

Glue up the sides

Once you've routed all the coves in the side pieces, you can begin gluing them up in pairs to create holes. Apply a single bead of glue carefully to each flat between the coves. Then clamp pairs together, aligning the coves; spring clamps apply more than enough pressure for this. After you've allowed the glue to dry on the pairs, remove the clamps and then glue up pairs of these as shown in the inset photo; repeat until one large block is formed.

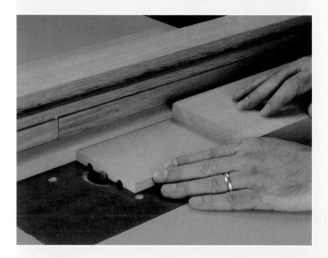

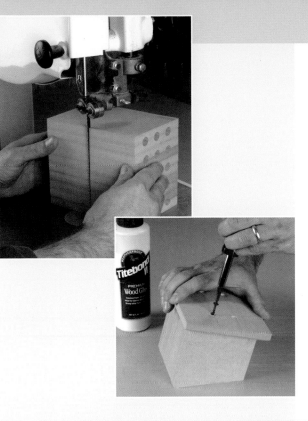

Cut the block in half

Scrape off any glue squeeze-out and then mark the block as shown in the angle detail in the drawing below. Although we used a band saw to cut the block in half at an angle, you could instead use a handsaw. Once it's cut, sand the cut edges smooth by hand or with a power sander.

Finishing touches

All that's left is to attach the base (as shown in the middle photo at left) and add labels (inset photo), or mark directly on the block with a pen. Depending on the number of blades you need to store, you may want to use both halves of the block for storage; see the sidebar below.

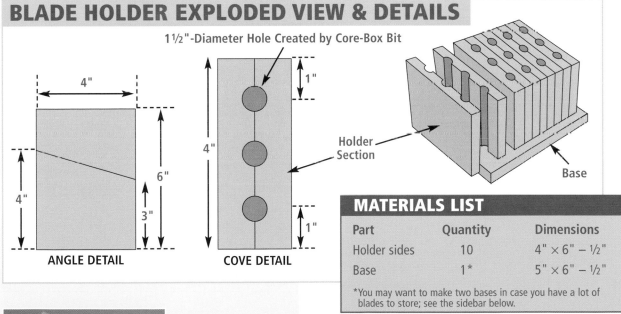

BLADE HOLDER EXPLODED VIEW & DETAILS

1½"-Diameter Hole Created by Core-Box Bit

4"

4"

6"

4"

3"

ANGLE DETAIL

4"

1"

1"

COVE DETAIL

Holder Section

Base

MATERIALS LIST

Part	Quantity	Dimensions
Holder sides	10	4" × 6" − ½"
Base	1*	5" × 6" − ½"

*You may want to make two bases in case you have a lot of blades to store; see the sidebar below.

TWICE THE STORAGE

You can make double the blade storage by making an additional base and attaching it to the top cutoff of the block. Alternatively, you can make one large base and attach both blocks to it as shown in the photo at left.

Knock-Down Scroll Seat

There's no doubt about it—scrolling is a lot more comfortable sitting down at a saw than it is standing up or bending over. The problem is, not everyone has a stool in the shop, and even if they do, it may not be the right height. What would be nice is a seat that's the perfect height, that doesn't take up any shop space, and that is comfortable. Our solution is a knock-down seat, shown here, that attaches to your saw stand.

Our seat is a simple design that requires only a few scraps of wood and some hinges; see the exploded view and materials list on the opposite page. When not in use, the seat folds down out of the way (see page 122). To use the seat, just lift it up—the support arm below locks in place to provide sturdy seating. *Warning:* Depending on the design of your stand, it may tilt forward on its front legs when someone sits on the knock-down seat. This is easily prevented by adding weight to the back of the stand; in most cases, a bag or two of play sand draped over the back leg brackets will create sufficient counterbalance to keep this from happening.

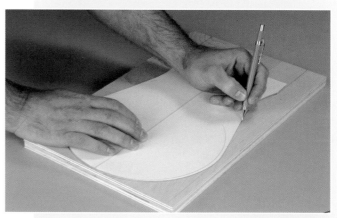

Trace pattern on seat blank
Use the pattern on the opposite page to create a seat template. Then place this on the seat blank and draw around it as shown in the middle photo. Alternatively, you can draw the seat shape directly on the blank; but you'll wish you had made a pattern when your buddies see the knock-down seat and they want to make their own.

Cut out seat
Next, cut out the seat shape with your scroll saw, as shown in the bottom photo. Then take the time now to round over the top edges of the seat—your bottom and inner thighs will thank you.

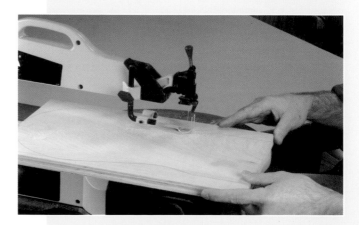

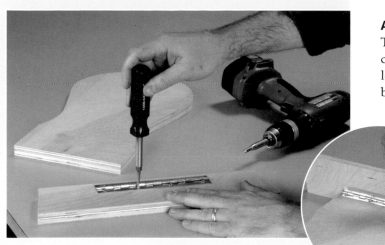

Attach the seat to the support cleat

The seat attaches to the upper support cleat by way of a piano hinge. The cleat is 3" wide and cut to length to fit your stand. You'll have to experiment a bit to find this length, since it will depend on where on the stand the seat will attach—which will define how high the seat is off the floor. For the Delta saw shown here, we positioned the seat 25" off the floor. Cut a piece of 1½"-wide piano hinge to a length of 8", and attach one hinge flap to the support cleat (top photo) and the other flap to the seat as shown in the inset photo.

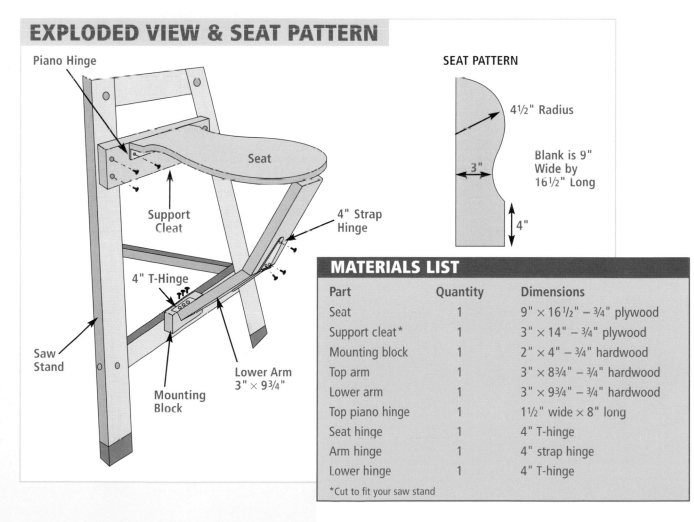

EXPLODED VIEW & SEAT PATTERN

Piano Hinge

Seat

Support Cleat

4" Strap Hinge

4" T-Hinge

Saw Stand

Mounting Block

Lower Arm 3" × 9¾"

SEAT PATTERN

4½" Radius

3"

Blank is 9" Wide by 16½" Long

4"

MATERIALS LIST

Part	Quantity	Dimensions
Seat	1	9" × 16½" − ¾" plywood
Support cleat*	1	3" × 14" − ¾" plywood
Mounting block	1	2" × 4" − ¾" hardwood
Top arm	1	3" × 8¾" − ¾" hardwood
Lower arm	1	3" × 9¾" − ¾" hardwood
Top piano hinge	1	1½" wide × 8" long
Seat hinge	1	4" T-hinge
Arm hinge	1	4" strap hinge
Lower hinge	1	4" T-hinge

*Cut to fit your saw stand

Connect the arms

The seat is supported in the open position by a pair of arms that are held together with a 4" strap hinge. Cut the top and lower arm to size and then butt the ends together. Position the hinge centered on the arms and drill pilot holes for the mounting screws. Then mount the hinge with the screws provided, as shown in the top photo.

Attach seat to saw

To attach the seat to your saw, you'll have to drill some holes in the stand. Start by holding the upper support cleat in place as shown in the middle photo, and mark locations on the stand for mounting holes. Drill pilot holes in the stand and secure the cleat to the stand with screws, making sure it's level.

Next, drill a pair of centered holes in the front lower stand bracket to mount the lower arm. Holding power for the screws is provided by a mounting block located behind the stand bracket. Attach the lower arm with screws as shown in the inset photo.

Finally, place the top arm under the seat so the seat is level. Make pilot holes through the seat hinge and attach the arm to the seat with screws.

USING THE KNOCK-DOWN SEAT

Open position. To use the knock-down seat, simply lift up on the seat until the support arms below the seat lock into place.

Closed position. The unique hinged support arms fold in half to tuck neatly inside the stand when the seat is lowered into the closed position.

Saw Stand with Storage

The saw stands that many manufacturers make for their saws leave something to be desired—built-in storage. Not only that, some stands put the saw at an uncomfortable working height. Add to this the cost of the stand, and it begins to make sense to build your own. The stand designed here features a slide-out drawer for storing blades, etc., plus simple construction and even a built-in angled footrest. (Folks who study ergonomics have shown that people sitting down experience less back fatigue if their feet are propped up at a slight angle.) The stand sides and back are joined with stub-tenon-and-groove joinery. This simple joinery technique allows you to glue in a panel to create a sturdy unit; see the exploded view and materials list on page 124.

Cut grooves in stiles and rails

To build the stand with storage, start by cutting the side and back stiles and rails to size. To join these parts together, you'll cut grooves in the stiles and rails, and stub tenons on the ends of the rails. Not only do the stub tenons fit in these grooves, but the actual panels do, too; see the joinery detail on page 125. You can cut the grooves on the router table with a straight bit or on the table saw with a dado or standard blade as shown in the middle photo. Adjust the blade and fence position to cut a centered $1/4" \times 1/4"$ groove along the long inside edges of the side stiles and rails. Use a featherboard to press the workpiece firmly against the fence to ensure an accurate cut.

Cut stub tenons on side rails

The next step is to cut tenons on the ends of the side and back rails to fit the grooves you just cut. Here again, these can be cut on the router table or on the table saw. The tenons should be centered on the thickness of the stock and $1/4"$ thick. You'll want to cut them just a hair under $1/4"$ long to provide room for glue. To prevent the ends of the rails from chipping out, make sure to use a backer board to push the workpiece past the blade, as shown in the bottom photo.

Cut grooves in side stiles for cross rails

The side panels are joined to the back and the front cross rails with a tongue-and-groove joint. It's easiest now to cut the grooves in the side stiles before the panels are assembled. The grooves are located $1/2$" in from the edge of the stiles; see the joinery detail in the drawing on page 125. The $1/4$" $\times$ $1/4$" grooves can be cut on the router table, on the table saw with a dado set, or on the table saw, taking multiple passes with a standard blade as shown in the top photo.

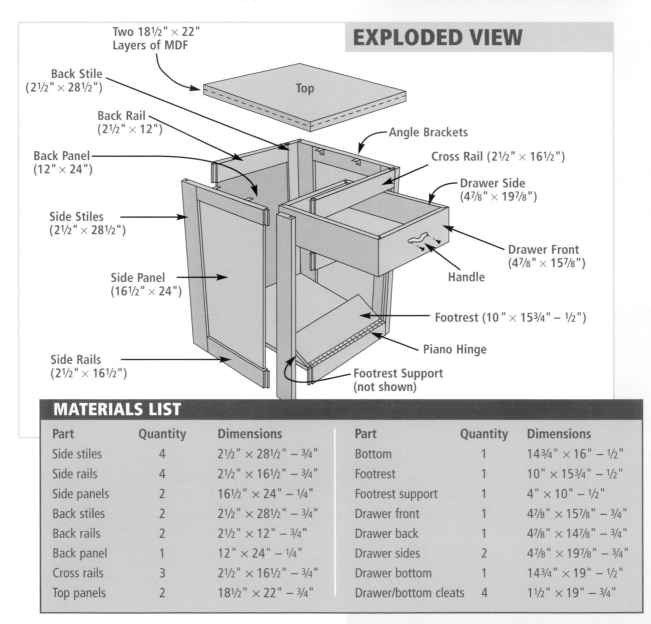

EXPLODED VIEW

Two 18½" × 22" Layers of MDF

Back Stile (2½" × 28½")

Back Rail (2½" × 12")

Back Panel (12" × 24")

Side Stiles (2½" × 28½")

Side Panel (16½" × 24")

Side Rails (2½" × 16½")

Top

Angle Brackets

Cross Rail (2½" × 16½")

Drawer Side (4⅞" × 19⅞")

Drawer Front (4⅞" × 15⅞")

Handle

Footrest (10 " × 15¾" − ½")

Piano Hinge

Footrest Support (not shown)

MATERIALS LIST

Part	Quantity	Dimensions	Part	Quantity	Dimensions
Side stiles	4	2½" × 28½" − ¾"	Bottom	1	14¾" × 16" − ½"
Side rails	4	2½" × 16½" − ¾"	Footrest	1	10" × 15¾" − ½"
Side panels	2	16½" × 24" − ¼"	Footrest support	1	4" × 10" − ½"
Back stiles	2	2½" × 28½" − ¾"	Drawer front	1	4⅞" × 15⅞" − ¾"
Back rails	2	2½" × 12" − ¾"	Drawer back	1	4⅞" × 14⅞" − ¾"
Back panel	1	12" × 24" − ¼"	Drawer sides	2	4⅞" × 19⅞" − ¾"
Cross rails	3	2½" × 16½" − ¾"	Drawer bottom	1	14¾" × 19" − ½"
Top panels	2	18½" × 22" − ¾"	Drawer/bottom cleats	4	1½" × 19" − ¾"

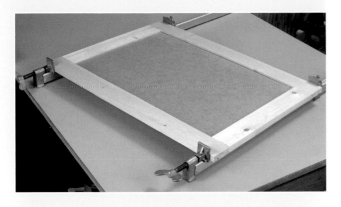

Glue up the sides and back

Once you've cut the grooves in the stiles, you can cut the panels to size from 1/4" hardboard and assemble each of the panels. Apply a generous bead of glue in the grooves cut into the edge of the stiles. Insert the stub tenon on a rail into the stile groove so that the bottom edges are flush, and insert a panel. Add the other rail and press the remaining stile in place. Clamp up the side as shown in the top photo. Check for square by measuring diagonals, and reposition the clamps if these numbers don't match. Repeat this for the second side and also the back.

Form tongues on cross rails and back

To form the tongues on the cross rails and back that fit into the grooves you cut earlier, cut a rabbet in the ends of the cross rails and along the length of the back stiles. Adjust the saw fence and blade to leave a 1/4" × 1/4" tongue, as shown in the middle photo. Again, use a backer board to prevent the cross rails from chipping out as you make the cut. Also, cut a 1/4" × 1/4" groove 1/2" down from the top inside face of one rail; this groove will accept a tongue cut on the bottom to hold it in place (see the footrest detail below).

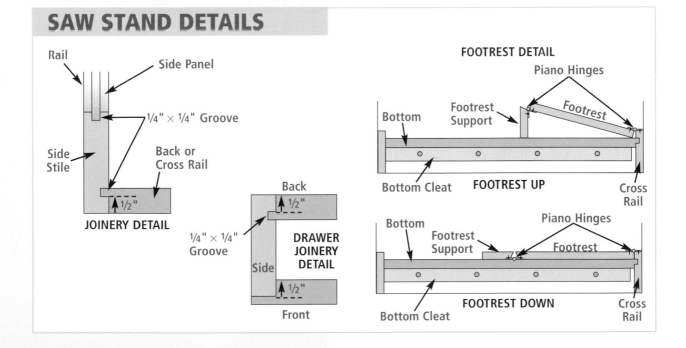

SAW STAND DETAILS

Rail

Side Panel

1/4" × 1/4" Groove

Side Stile

Back or Cross Rail

1/2"

JOINERY DETAIL

1/4" × 1/4" Groove

Back

1/2"

Side

DRAWER JOINERY DETAIL

1/2"

Front

FOOTREST DETAIL

Piano Hinges

Bottom

Footrest Support

Footrest

Bottom Cleat

FOOTREST UP

Cross Rail

Bottom

Piano Hinges

Footrest Support

Footrest

Bottom Cleat

FOOTREST DOWN

Cross Rail

Glue up stand

Now you can assemble the stand. It's a good idea to dry-assemble all the parts without glue first to make sure everything fits together as it should. When it does, disassemble the parts of the stand and apply a bead of glue in the rear grooves cut into faces of the sides that will accept the full-length tongue of the back. Insert the back between the sides and apply clamps. Apply glue to the tongues on the cross rails, and insert these in the grooves in the front of the stand. One rail is flush with the top of the sides, the grooved rail is installed flush with the bottom of the sides with the groove facing in, and the remaining cross rail is located 5" down from the bottom of the top cross rail as shown in the top photo. This last rail forms the opening for the drawer, added later.

Add the top

To add weight to the stand and create a solid foundation for mounting the saw, the top is made up of two $^3/_4$" layers of medium-density fiberboard (MDF) that are glued and screwed together. Once the glue dries, the top can be attached to the cabinet; it connects to the cabinet via a set of four angle brackets, as shown in the inset photo. The easiest way to mount the top is to attach the brackets, position the top on a work surface, and flip the stand upside down on top of it. This way you can reach in easily and screw the top to the brackets, as shown in the middle photo.

Assemble the footrest

The footrest is optional; see the detail on page 125 to see how it operates inside the stand. If you plan to add it, cut the footrest and footrest support to size. Connect the two parts with a length of piano hinge using the screws provided, as shown in the bottom photo. You'll also want to cut the bottom to size at this time and cut a $^1/_4$" tongue on its front edge to fit in the groove in the bottom cross rail you cut earlier. Install the bottom and then position one bottom cleat under each side of the bottom. Screw these cleats to the sides to support the bottom (these are similar to the cleats you'll install later to support the drawer; see page 128 for more on this).

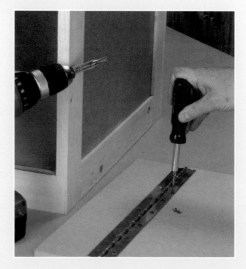

Attach footrest to cabinet

Once you've connected the halves of the footrest, you can attach it to the cabinet. Since the parts of the footrest were cut from $1/2$"-thick stock and you grooved the bottom cross rail $1/2$" down from its top edge, this will create a $1/2$" space for the footrest. Attach one flap of a 10"-long piano hinge on the unattached end of the footrest. Then position the footrest inside the stand so that the remaining hinge flap is flat on the top edge of the bottom cross rail. Attach the hinge flap to the cross rail with the screws provided, as shown in the top photo.

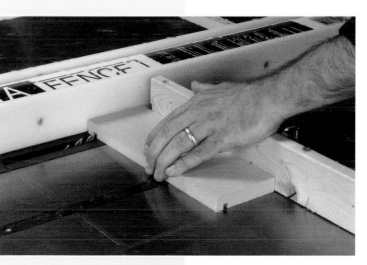

Cut grooves in drawer sides

All that's left is to make the storage drawer and add the cleats that support it. To make the drawer, start by cutting the drawer parts to size; see the materials list on page 124. The sides of the drawer connect to the drawer front with a simple rabbet joint, the back is joined to the sides with a locking rabbet joint; and the bottom fits in grooves cut into the front, back, and sides of the drawer; see the drawer joinery detail on page 125. Cut $1/4$" × $1/4$" grooves in the back of each side $1/2$" in from the end, as shown in the middle photo.

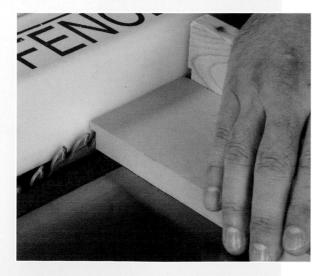

Cut tenons in the drawer front/back

Next you can cut rabbets on both ends of the back piece to form a tongue to fit in the grooves you just cut in the sides. Adjust the rip fence and saw blade to create a tongue that's $1/4$" thick and just slightly less than $1/4$" long to allow clearance for glue, as shown in the bottom photo.

Cut grooves for drawer bottom

Finally, cut a $1/4" \times 1/4"$ groove $1/4"$ up from the bottom edge of the front, back, and sides as shown in the top photo. This groove will accept the tongue that's cut on the drawer bottom. Since the drawer bottom is $1/2"$ thick, you'll need to rabbet the edges to create a tongue that's $1/4"$ thick and just slightly less than $1/4"$ long for glue clearance.

Glue up drawer

With all the joinery complete on the drawer parts, you can assemble the drawer. Start by applying a bead of glue to the grooves cut in the front, back, and sides for the bottom. Then apply glue to the grooves near the back edge of the sides. Insert the back into one of the sides and then slip in the bottom. Add the remaining side and press on the front. Apply clamps as shown in the middle photo, and measure diagonals to check for square. If the measurements aren't the same, adjust the clamps and repeat measuring and adjust until they're equal.

Attach drawer cleats

The drawer slides in and out of the stand on a pair of drawer cleats that are attached to the inside faces of the side panels. Set the stand on its side and position a cleat inside the stand so it's flush with the top of the middle cross rail. Level the cleat and attach it to the sides with screws as shown in the bottom photo; repeat for the other side. Apply a few coats of polyurethane to the stand, and install a handle or pull in the drawer front.

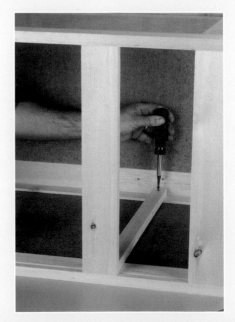

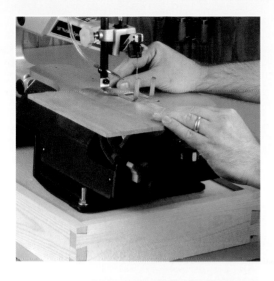

Sand-Filled Saw Base

Any scroller who's ever used a bench-top scroll saw knows that it needs to be mounted securely to a work surface to keep it from sliding around in use. Clamping the saw in place will help prevent it from sliding around, but it won't help dampen vibration. And most bench-top scroll saws that aren't permanently mounted to a stand will vibrate in use. This vibration doesn't help you make an accurate cut while you try to steer a workpiece along a line. That's why the base offered here keeps your bench-top saw from sliding around and dampens vibration. The secret to this base is what's hidden inside—sand. Sand adds weight and does a terrific job of eliminating vibration problems. To contain this heavy sand, we needed to join the sides together with a strong mechanical joint—that's why we chose dovetails; see the exploded view and materials list on page 130.

Lay out tails on front and back

Begin work on the sand-filled base by cutting the front, back, and sides of the base to size. Note that the base described here fits the Ryobi saw shown in the top photo. You can easily modify the length of the front, back, and sides to fit your saw. Just measure the width and length of the saw's base and add 3" to 4" for clearance on the sides. Once you've cut the parts to length and width, lay out the tails on the sides. We used a dovetail gauge for this (middle photo), but a sliding bevel works just as well; see the dovetail detail in the drawing on page 130.

Cut out tails

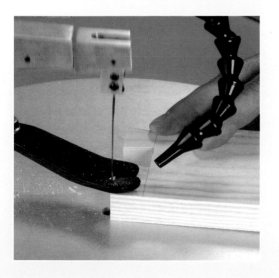

Once the tails are laid out, they can be cut out on the scroll saw. Double-check that the saw's table is set for a 90-degree cut, and make the cuts to define the sides of the tails first, as shown in the bottom photo. Make sure to stay just to the waste side of the marked lines. Then go back and cut the bottoms of the tails to remove the waste between each tail. Here again, stay on the waste side of the line. You can always go back and trim these to the line with a sharp chisel.

Use tails to lay out pins

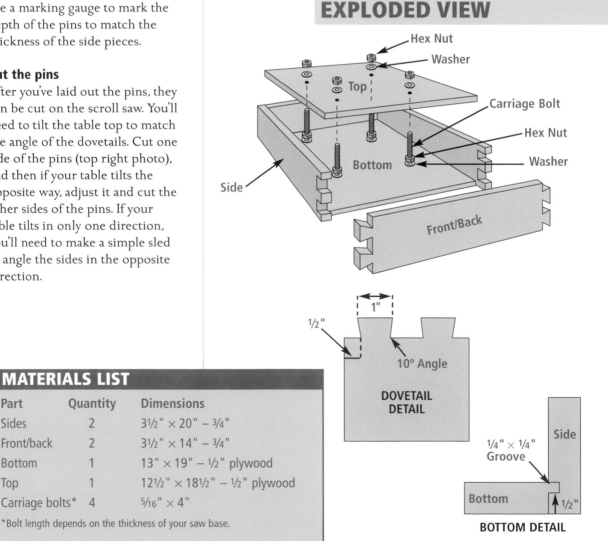

Once you've cut the tails and trimmed them as needed, you can use these to lay out the pins in the sides. To do this, first lay out the parts as they'll be when assembled, and mark each so you team up the right tails with the corresponding pins. Then pick one corner and lay the side piece flat on the work surface. Position the tail piece on end as shown in the top left photo, and use an awl or pencil to transfer the locations of the sides of the tails to the ends of the side pieces. Use a small try square to continue these lines onto the faces of the sides. Then use a marking gauge to mark the depth of the pins to match the thickness of the side pieces.

Cut the pins

After you've laid out the pins, they can be cut on the scroll saw. You'll need to tilt the table top to match the angle of the dovetails. Cut one side of the pins (top right photo), and then if your table tilts the opposite way, adjust it and cut the other sides of the pins. If your table tilts in only one direction, you'll need to make a simple sled to angle the sides in the opposite direction.

EXPLODED VIEW

Hex Nut
Washer
Top
Carriage Bolt
Hex Nut
Washer
Bottom
Side
Front/Back

DOVETAIL DETAIL

1"
1/2"
10° Angle

BOTTOM DETAIL

Side
1/4" × 1/4" Groove
Bottom
1/2"

MATERIALS LIST

Part	Quantity	Dimensions
Sides	2	3½" × 20" – ¾"
Front/back	2	3½" × 14" – ¾"
Bottom	1	13" × 19" – ½" plywood
Top	1	12½" × 18½" – ½" plywood
Carriage bolts*	4	5⁄16" × 4"

*Bolt length depends on the thickness of your saw base.

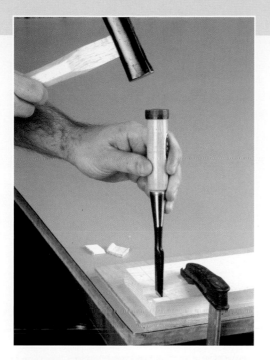

Remove waste between pins

The simplest way to remove the waste between the sides of the pins is to cut them out with a chisel. Clamp the sides onto a scrap piece and use a mallet and a chisel to sever the waste between the pin sides as shown in the top photo. Take care to chisel only halfway through. Then flip the workpiece and remove the remaining waste. This method ensures that the bottom edges where the tails will fit will be square on both faces.

Cut grooves for bottom

The bottom of the base is a piece of $1/2$" plywood that's rabbeted around its edges to form a tongue (inset photo) that fits in grooves cut in the front, back, and sides; see the bottom detail in the drawing on page 130. The groove for the bottom is $1/4" \times 1/4"$ and is located $1/4"$ up from the bottom edge of the front, back, and sides. You can cut these grooves on the router table or the table saw as shown in the middle photo. Note that cutting these grooves in the front and back will cut into the bottom edge of the lower tails. These small square holes can be filled with wood plugs once the base is assembled.

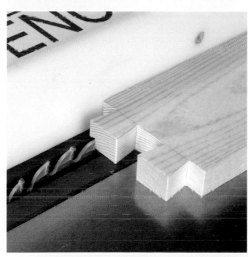

Assemble the base

Once the grooves have been cut for the bottom and it has been rabbeted, you can assemble the base. Apply a bead of glue in the grooves for the bottom. Then apply glue sparingly to one of the sets of tails and pins and tap them together with a mallet. Slide the bottom into the grooves and add the other side, followed by the remaining front/back piece. Apply clamps to the base and allow the glue to dry overnight as shown in the bottom photo. While the glue is drying, cut a top to fit inside the base.

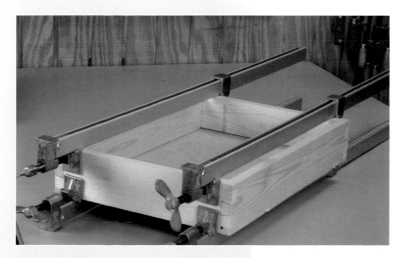

Drill mounting holes

The saw is mounted to the base by way of four carriage bolts that fit in counterbored holes in the bottom. The bolts also pass through the top, so it's important that you locate and drill these all at the same time. Start by placing the saw on the top, and center it from side to side and from back to back. Use a pencil to mark through the saw's mounting holes onto the top, and then remove the saw, as shown in the top photo. Then slip the top into the base so that it lies flat on the bottom and drill mounting holes through both layers at the same time (inset photo).

Add bolts to base

Remove the top from inside the base and flip the base over. Counterbore each hole location so that the head of the carriage bolt won't protrude past the bottom. Now you can insert the bolts and flip the base right side up. To hold the bolts in place inside the base, slip washers over each bolt and then thread on nuts. Spin them all the way down and tighten them with a wrench, as shown in the middle photo.

Fill with sand and add saw

All that's left is to fill the base with sand, add the top, and mount the saw. Make sure your sand is dry, and carefully pour some into the base, stopping frequently to level it (bottom photo). When you get near the top edge of the front, back, and sides, stop and add the top and saw. Thread on washers and nuts, and tighten the bolts as shown in the inset photo. Plug in the saw and let it run for a few minutes to compact the sand. Retighten the bolts and repeat until the sand is fully compacted and you can't tighten the bolts any further. Now you can scroll away, knowing vibration will no longer be a problem.

Pantograph

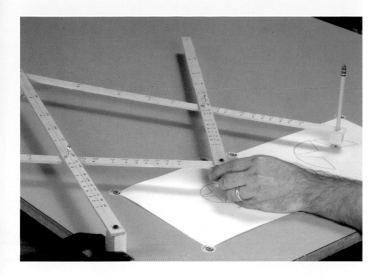

So you're ready to get scrolling on a new project and you realize that the pattern you want to use is too small or too big. What do you do? For most folks this means a trip to the nearest office-supply store or library to use their copy machine. You stop working, brush the sawdust off your clothes, and drive there, only to discover their copy machine can't enlarge or reduce. Frustrated, you drive back home bemoaning the precious shop time you've just lost. A simpler, inexpensive solution is to do your own enlargements and reductions at home. Can't afford a copier that does this? No problem. Just make the easy-to-use pantograph shown here. A pantograph is just a set of strips of wood that can be connected to each other in various positions to provide different ratios for making your own patterns; see the exploded view and materials list on page 134. This accordion-like contraption is easy to use: Just follow your original pattern with the scribe, and the pencil on the end strip will draw a larger or smaller pattern.

Cut the strips to size

Begin work on the pantograph by cutting the wood strips to size. You'll need four of these strips; cut them from seasoned hardwood so they'll stay flat over time. To prevent the thin strips from falling down into the opening in your table saw's insert, make sure to use a zero-clearance insert when cutting them, as shown in the middle photo.

Draw a center reference line

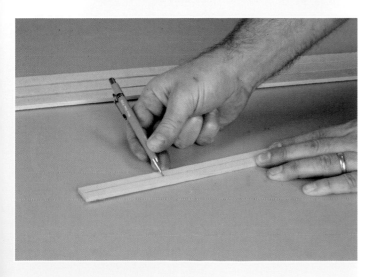

The only challenging part to making the pantograph is that you need to be exacting in your layout of the holes in the strips. These holes are used later to attach the strips together to create the various enlargement and reduction ratios. To identify each of the four strips, letter them on the face side from A to D. Mark the A and C strips on the left-hand end and the B and D strips on the right-hand end. Then draw a centered line down the full length of the A strip as shown in the bottom photo.

Lay out the hole locations

Next, lay out the hole locations on this centerline, starting from the right-hand end. Start by measuring ¹⁄₂" in from the end and make a mark. Then lay out the remaining hole locations as shown in the strip hole location detail on page 135. Take your time here, and double-check your measurements for accuracy once you've made all your marks.

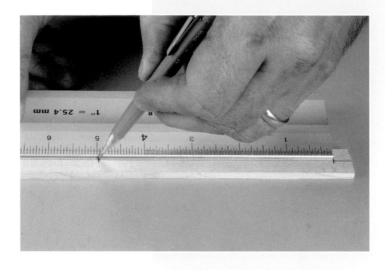

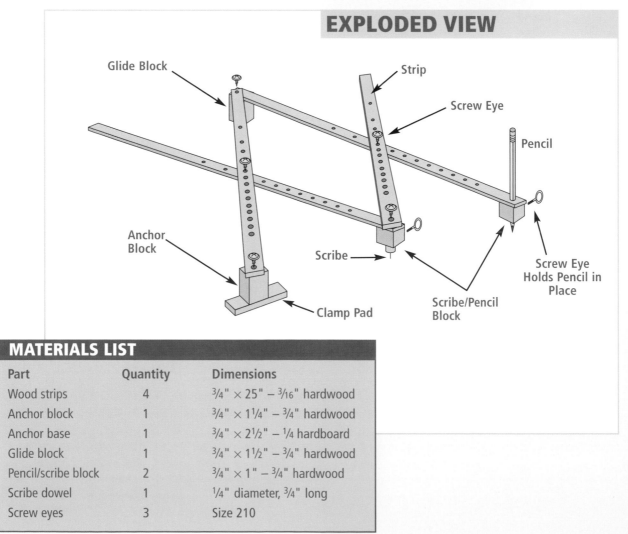

EXPLODED VIEW

Glide Block

Strip

Screw Eye

Pencil

Anchor Block

Scribe

Screw Eye Holds Pencil in Place

Scribe/Pencil Block

Clamp Pad

MATERIALS LIST

Part	Quantity	Dimensions
Wood strips	4	³⁄₄" × 25" − ³⁄₁₆" hardwood
Anchor block	1	³⁄₄" × 1¹⁄₄" − ³⁄₄" hardwood
Anchor base	1	³⁄₄" × 2¹⁄₂" − ¹⁄₄ hardboard
Glide block	1	³⁄₄" × 1¹⁄₂" − ³⁄₄" hardwood
Pencil/scribe block	2	³⁄₄" × 1" − ³⁄₄" hardwood
Scribe dowel	1	¹⁄₄" diameter, ³⁄₄" long
Screw eyes	3	Size 210

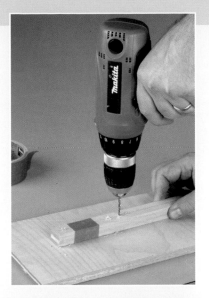

Drill the pivot holes

Once you've marked all the hole locations on the strips, you can start drilling. Gather the strips together with the A and C letters on the left and the B and D letters on the right. Then with the A strip on top, wrap some masking tape around the ends to clamp the strips together as shown in the top photo. Using a ⅛" bit, drill all 16 holes in the strips. A drill press is the best tool for this job; but if you don't have one, a portable drill will work. Just remember to protect your work surface by inserting a scrap of wood between the strips and the work surface.

Reclamp and drill shank holes

Remove the masking tape and separate the strips. Then gather the A and C strips back together and wrap the ends with masking tape. Now enlarge all holes with a 5/32" bit as shown in the middle photo. This extra 1/32" provides clearance for the shanks of the screw eyes that connect the strips together. It also allows the A and C strips to pivot freely—something that's quite necessary for the pantograph to operate smoothly.

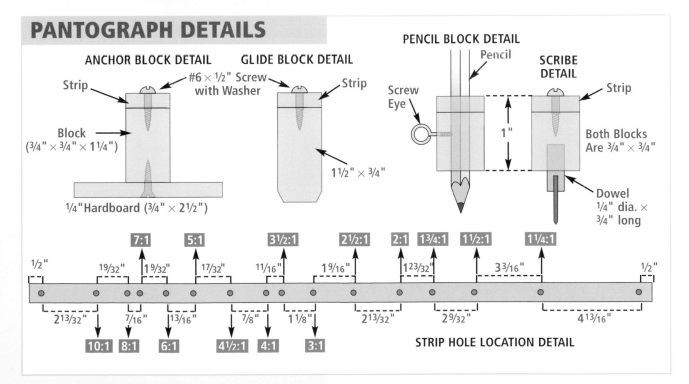

PANTOGRAPH DETAILS

ANCHOR BLOCK DETAIL — GLIDE BLOCK DETAIL — PENCIL BLOCK DETAIL — SCRIBE DETAIL

STRIP HOLE LOCATION DETAIL

Label pivot holes

With holes in the A and C strips enlarged, you can label each of the holes in the strips with ratio numbers, as shown in the top photo. The ratio locations are illustrated in the strip hole location drawing on the bottom of page 135. A permanent marker like a Sharpie brand works best for this, as the numbers can't wear off over time.

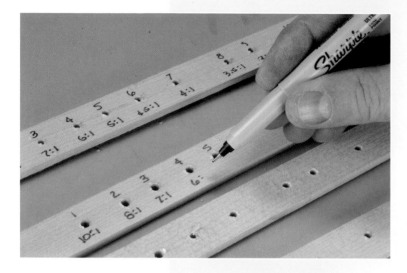

Attach glide block

The strips are almost complete at this point. All that's left is to make the various blocks that attach to their ends, and attach them. Start by cutting the glide block to size—it's just a scrap of hardwood that's 3/4" square and 1 1/2" long. This block supports the far end of the pantograph in use and is attached to the end of the B strip as shown in the middle photo. Because the block doesn't need to pivot, you can glue it onto the strip. Later, the A strip is attached to the B strip and glide block with a small screw.

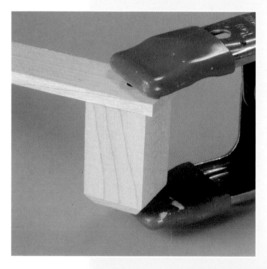

Make the pencil holder

Next you can turn your attention to the pencil holder. This is a scrap of hardwood with a hole drilled in it to accept a pencil; the pencil is held in place by a screw eye that passes through the side of the pencil block and into the pencil; see the pencil block detail on page 135. The pencil block is 3/4" square and 1" long. Drill a 1/4" hole the length of the block as shown in the bottom photo. Then drill a small pilot hole through the side for the screw eye, and screw the eye into the block.

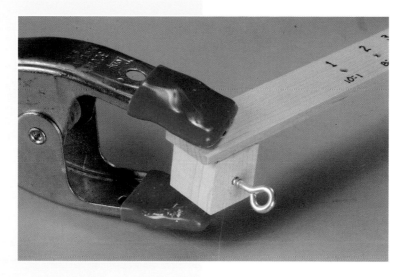

Attach the pencil block

Now you can glue the pencil block to the end of the B strip opposite the glide block you attached earlier, as shown in the top photo. When the glue is dry, you'll need to use a ¼" bit to drill through the pencil block and the B strip to allow the pencil to pass through the B strip. Slip a pencil in place and secure it by tightening the screw eye.

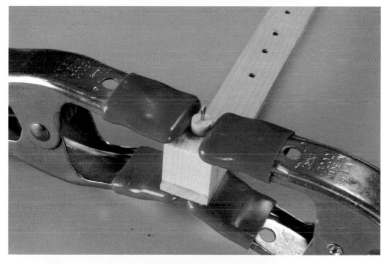

Make and attach scribe

The scribe block is also a scrap of hardwood that is ¾" square and 1" long. Instead of a pencil, it holds a shop-made scribe. This is nothing more than a short length of ¼" dowel with a nail inserted in its end; see the scribe detail drawing on page 135. Glue the nail into the end of the dowel with epoxy and then glue the scribe into the scribe block. Next, glue and clamp the scribe block onto the end of the D strip as shown in the middle photo. Note: To prevent the scribe from scratching or tearing your original pattern in use, file a slight roundover on the end of the nail.

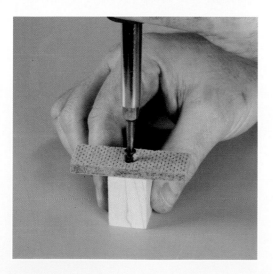

Make the anchor block

The anchor block holds the pantograph in place during use. It consists of two parts: a ¾"-square × 1¼"-long block, and a ¾" × 2½"-long hardboard base. Cut these parts to size and then assemble them with glue and a single screw as shown in the bottom photo. Attach this block to the unmarked end of the A strip with a washer and a #6 × ⅝" woodscrew.

Attach glide block

To assemble the pantograph, start by positioning the unattached end of the A strip to the B strip and the glide block. Secure these together at the end with a washer and a #6 × ⁵⁄₈" woodscrew as shown in the top photo.

Attach strips to scribe and pencil blocks

Continue assembly by positioning the C strip over the D strip and securing the ends to the scribe block with a washer and a #6 × ⁵⁄₈" woodscrew as shown in the middle photo. Then place the C strip over the B strip at the desired ratio and connect with a screw eye; position the A strip over the D strip at the desired ratio and connect with the remaining screw eye.

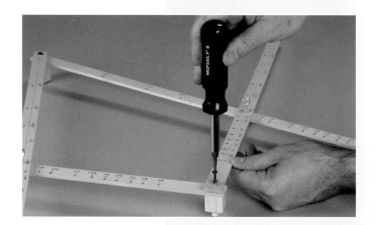

USING THE PANTOGRAPH

The pantograph can be used to either enlarge or reduce a pattern. To enlarge a pattern, use the pantograph as described here. If you want to reduce a pattern, you'll need to swap the B strip with the D strip so that the pencil and scribe are reversed. This way when you trace the original, the pencil will draw a smaller pattern.

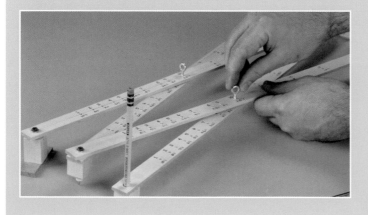

Adjust strips for desired ratio. The first thing to do to enlarge a pattern is to set up the pantograph for the desired enlargement ratio. To do this, simply align the same ratio number in all four strips and connect the strips with the screw eyes as shown in the photo at left.

Clamp the anchor block in place. Next, you'll want to mount the pantograph to a large, flat work surface. Use a clamp or two to secure the anchor block to the edge of the work surface as shown in the top photo. Make sure you've got plenty of elbow room both to the right and to the left of the pantograph for the strips to move as the pantograph traces the pattern.

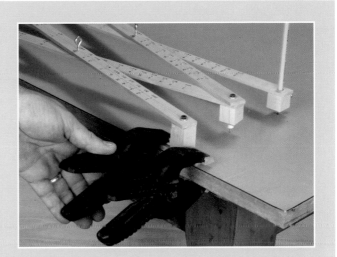

Set up the pattern and paper. All that's left is to set up the pattern and the blank paper for your new pattern. Compress the pantograph as much as possible and then slip the pattern under the scribe so the left edge of the pattern is under the scribe and centered on it from top to bottom. Secure the pattern to the work surface with masking tape or drafting dots as shown in the middle photo. Then insert a blank sheet of paper under the pencil so the left edge of the paper is about 1" to the left of the pencil and the paper is centered from top to bottom on the pencil. Secure the blank sheet with masking tape or drafting dots.

Trace original to enlarge. Now you can enlarge your pattern. Place light pressure on the scribe and trace the pattern as shown in the bottom photo. The pencil should draw a correspondingly large pattern on your blank sheet. If it doesn't, you may need to adjust the pencil's position. Also, be aware that anytime you move the scribe, the pencil will draw a matching line. So if you want to move the scribe to another part of the pattern to trace, you should lift the pencil so it doesn't draw a line across your new pattern.

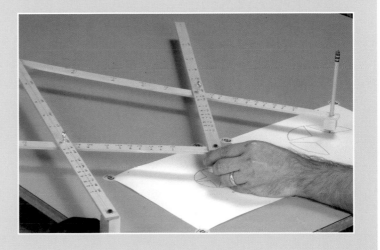

70490

3-IN-ONE
MULTI-PURPOSE
OIL
LUBRICATES, CLEANS
& PREVENTS RUST
DANGER
3 FL OZ

OPERATOR'S MANUAL
RYOBI.
16 in. (406 mm) Variable Speed
SCROLL SAW
Model SC164VS

Reduce
Friction & He
CT
Cutting Tool L
· prolongs tool life
· seals and lubricates
by penetrating and bo
to tool surface
· no effect on finishing o
· non-toxic
OLV
8 FL OZ

HEGNER
Universal Precision Saws

For all powe
Saw

rbi
MADE IN
USA

rbi
OPERATORS MANUAL

MODELS 216, 220 & 226
HAWK ULTRAS

INSTRUCTI

16" Variable Speed Scroll Saw
with Quickset II® Blade
Changing Feature
(Models SS350, SS350LS)

DELTA

MANUAL #

P
Copyrig

6 Maintenance & Troubleshooting

Although simple to use, the average scroll saw has many moving parts that require periodic maintenance. But despite the number of parts, the maintenance involved is neither complicated nor time-consuming. All it takes to keep a scroll saw running in tip-top condition is some cleaning and lubrication supplies, a hand tool or two, and an afternoon. In just a few hours you can give your saw a top-to-bottom overhaul that will keep it running smoothly for future projects.

This chapter reviews the basic parts of your saw and shows you what parts need lubricating, how to lubricate them, and what lubricant to use. Then there are guidelines on table-top maintenance, common electrical repairs, blade maintenance and modification, and finally, how to troubleshoot common scrolling problems.

The owner's manual for your scroll saw is your best guide for maintenance and troubleshooting. With a few simple supplies and hand tools, you can have your saw running at peak performance in no time.

Basic Saw Anatomy

The anatomy of a scroll saw will depend primarily on its type. Since the most common type of scroll saw used today is the parallel-arm saw, we'll describe that here.

The foundation of any scroll saw is its base. In most cases, this is a single piece made of cast iron to provide weight for vibration-dampening; see the exploded view drawing below. Typically, a motor support and bracket attach to this base to hold the motor and support the back end of the saw table. A trunion attaches to the front of the motor support and connects to the underside of the table so the table can be tilted. The tilt lock control locks the trunion—and table—in at the desired angle.

The saw table is usually cast iron, but may be cast or machined aluminum. An opening in the table allows blade changes, and the opening is reduced by a drop-in table insert. The motor, starter capacitor, and switch box, which contains the saw's wiring and speed and on/off switches, attach to the motor support. The side covers

contain and support the saw's upper and lower arms and link that connects to the motor's drive shaft.

The hold-down assembly, consisting of the blade guard and hold-down, attach to a post housed in one of the side covers. The blade clamp assemblies connect to the ends of the upper and lower arm. These consist of the blade clamp pads, some form of release mechanism and, in the saw shown here, the tension adjustment and release as well.

A diaphragm rests below or above one of the arms and is compressed when the arms move up and down to produce airflow. This air runs through plastic tubing up to the end of the upper arm and attaches to an articulated arm that lets the operator position the arm as needed to keep the kerf clean.

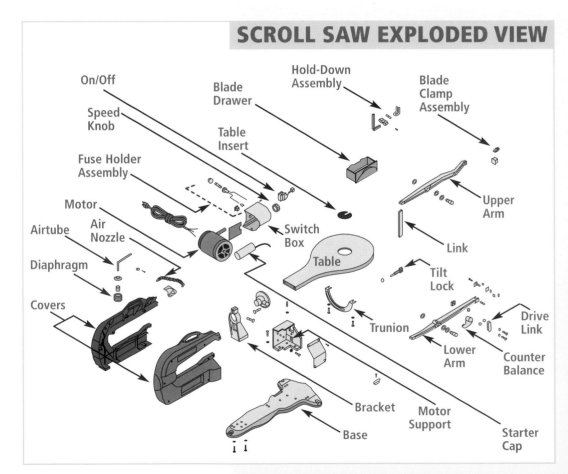

SCROLL SAW EXPLODED VIEW

On/Off · Speed Knob · Fuse Holder Assembly · Motor · Airtube · Air Nozzle · Diaphragm · Covers · Blade Drawer · Table Insert · Hold-Down Assembly · Blade Clamp Assembly · Switch Box · Table · Upper Arm · Link · Tilt Lock · Drive Link · Lower Arm · Counter Balance · Trunion · Bracket · Motor Support · Base · Starter Cap

Lubrication

Besides keeping your scroll saw clean, the number one thing you can do to it to keep it running smooth and trouble-free over the years is to lubricate it frequently. Because of the inherent up-and-down motion of the arms, there are a lot of moving parts that require constant lubrication to prevent problems. Consult your owner's manual for recommended lubrication points and the recommended lubricant. In many cases, manufacturers recommend lubricating the saw after every 20 hours of use.

Lubrication points

The drawing below left illustrates the typical lubrication points on a scroll saw. The most important lubrication points are those of the linkages of the upper and lower arms. Additionally, because there are so many parts of the blade mechanisms that pivot or move, these also require constant cleaning and lubrication. The table top itself will also benefit from a little TLC from time to time (for more on table-top maintenance, see pages 148–149).

Clean before lubricating

If there's one thing that most experienced woodworkers have learned about tool maintenance over the years, it's to clean a tool before applying a lubricant. Compressed air—from either a shop compressor or a can—will make quick work of blowing away dust and dirt inside a saw. Pay particular attention to the upper and lower arm pivot points as shown in the top photo. Any dust that mixes with lubricant can sneak inside the sleeve bearing and slowly grind metal to create a loose pivot point.

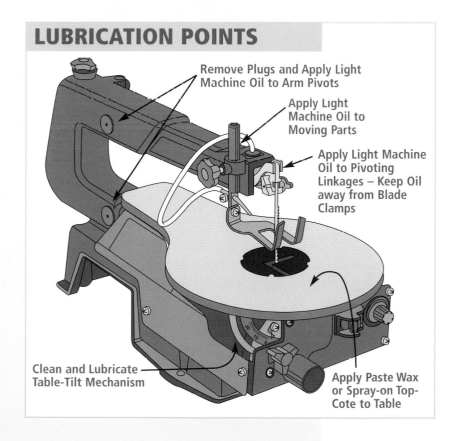

LUBRICATION POINTS

Remove Plugs and Apply Light Machine Oil to Arm Pivots

Apply Light Machine Oil to Moving Parts

Apply Light Machine Oil to Pivoting Linkages – Keep Oil away from Blade Clamps

Clean and Lubricate Table-Tilt Mechanism

Apply Paste Wax or Spray-on Top-Cote to Table

ACCESSING PIVOT POINTS

The ease with which you can access the pivot points of the upper and lower arms will depend on the manufacturer of the saw. On some saws, you can remove one or both of the side covers; others offer pry-off caps that make access easy (see below).

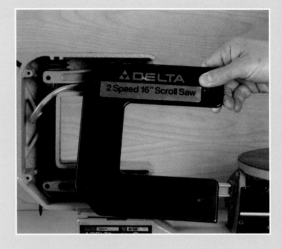

No caps. Many older scroll saws do not have any plugs or caps that can be removed to access the pivot points for lubrication. On these saws, you'll have to remove one or both of the side covers as shown in the photo at right. This might seem like a disadvantage, but it really isn't. That's because you'll want to lubricate more than just the pivot points. For example, the drive linkages (page 145) need frequent lubrication as well—and you have to remove the side covers anyway to access these.

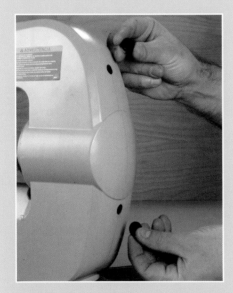

Rear caps. Newer saws, like the Delta scroll saw shown in the middle photo, have a set of pry-out plugs in the back of the saw that provide lubrication access to the arm pivot points. These rubber caps are easily pried off with a flat-blade screwdriver. Make sure to follow the manufacturer's recommendations for lubricating these points. In many cases, all they call for is a few drops of oil. Don't get carried away here; more is not better. Excess oil will drip down inside the casing and eventually work itself out onto your bench or stand.

Side caps. Other saw manufacturers provide access to the pivot points on the sides of the saw. Again, pry-out rubber caps are usually used. Once you've pried them out, it's best to rest the saw on its side as shown in the bottom photo so that gravity can help the light machine oil travel down into the pivot point. Wipe off any excess oil and press the caps back in place.

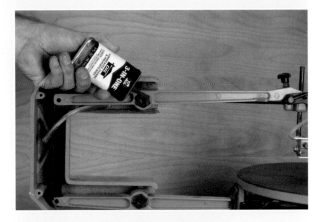

Lubricate the pivot points

How you access the pivot points on your saw will depend on the manufacturer; see the sidebar on page 144 for more on this. Once you've accessed the pivot points, a light machine oil will do just fine for lubricating the pivot points of the upper and lower arms on most saws. Carefully apply some oil to each pivot, and then manually move the arms up and down to distribute the oil, as shown in the top photo. Apply a little more oil and repeat the up-and-down motion. Wipe off any excess oil: This will act as a magnet for dust and will quickly turn into an oil/dust goo that will only cause problems.

Lubricate the drive linkages

In addition to the main pivot points for the upper and lower arms, it's a good idea to routinely lubricate the drive linkages that connect the arms, as shown in the middle photo. You may or may not have to remove the side covers to access these points. The drive linkages aren't under anywhere near the stress that the pivot points are, so they don't require lubrication as frequently as the pivot point. Every 40 hours of use or so will do just fine.

Motor drive link

If your motor drive linkages are exposed once you've taken the side covers off, take the time to apply a few drops of light machine oil to the linkage that connects the motor shaft to the lower arms, as shown in the bottom photo. This pivot point gets as much action as the pivot points for the arms and will certainly benefit from frequent lubrication. Remember: If there's no oil between the moving parts, the parts will quickly start grinding away on each other. The end result will be a sloppy fit and increased vibration.

Lubricate the blade linkages

There are a number of exposed moving parts near the upper arm that will benefit from frequent attention, especially the blade guard/hold-down assembly and the blade linkages. Blow out both of these with compressed air, and apply a drop or two of light machine oil to the post where the guard/hold-down assembly moves up and down. Additionally, apply a few drops of oil to the pivot points of the blade linkages as shown in the top photo. Take care not to get any on the clamp pads themselves, as this can cause blade slippage.

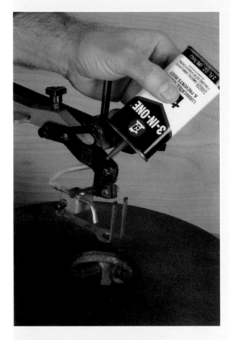

Table pivot points

Finally, you'll want to lubricate the points where the table top pivots. The front pivot point is easily accessible. Just apply a few drops to the pivot located under the front of the table top, as shown in the middle photo. Apply the oil to the pivot point and not the trunion. If you lubricate the trunion, the oil may cause it to shift out of place when the table-tilt lock is engaged.

To access the back pivot point for the table, you'll usually need to loosen the table-tilt lock and tilt the table to its maximum angle as shown in the bottom photo. This will expose the pivot point so you can get in with an oil can. Just a drop or two is all it takes here because this is not a major moving part. As always, wipe up any excess oil to prevent sawdust/oil goo from forming.

Performance Tests

Once your scroll saw is clean and lubricated, it's a good idea to make a couple of quick tests to check its performance.

Table alignment

There are a couple of quick ways to make sure your table is perpendicular to the blade. The first is to simply place a try square (a small engineer's square like the one shown in the top photo works great for this) up against the blade. Any gap between the square and the blade indicates a misalignment. Another way to check a table without using a try square is to make a shallow kerf on the edge of a board. Then rotate the workpiece with the same surface flat on the saw table so the kerf you just cut ends up behind the blade. If the blade is aligned with the kerf, the blade is perpendicular to the table. If it isn't aligned, the table is out of adjustment.

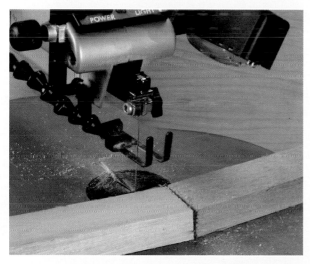

You can also check the table blade alignment by crosscutting a piece of scrap in half, as shown in the middle photo. Flip one of the pieces over and butt the ends together. Any variation from 90 degrees will be doubled and easy to see. No angle variation between the two ends means the table is exactly 90 degrees to the blade.

Blade drift

If you've ever noticed that you have to angle a workpiece to follow a straight line, you've experienced blade drift. Blade drift is caused by improper milling of the teeth. What happens is that as the teeth are ground, a burr is formed on one side of the blade. This causes the blade to pull to one side or the other as it cuts. The only thing you can do about this is replace the blade. To check for drift, ease a workpiece gently into the running blade with light pressure as shown in the bottom photo. If the workpiece tracks to one side or the other, the blade is burred and should be replaced.

Maintaining the Table Top

For best results when scrolling, your workpiece should lie flat on the saw top and glide effortlessly across it as you make your cuts. For this to happen, you need to periodically maintain the top.

Leveling

It's smart to occasionally check to make sure that your saw top is flat and level. Place a straightedge on the top from side to side, from back to front, and on both diagonals, and check for gaps under the straightedge. If you find gaps, mark the high spots and level these with a sanding block wrapped with emery cloth or silicon-carbide sandpaper, as shown in the top photo. For large variations, you'll have to take the top to a machine shop for flattening. Note: Anytime you plan to do anything to your saw top, you should start by cleaning it with a clean cloth dipped in solvent such as acetone to remove any old sealant or other impurities. (Always first check your solvent in an inconspicuous place to make sure that it won't damage the top.)

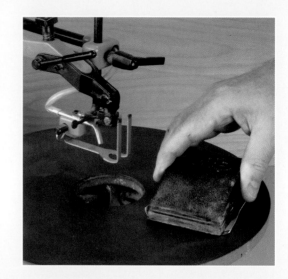

Smoothing

Once the top has been leveled, it's good practice to smooth the entire top by first removing any rust spots or other buildups on your table top. You can switch to a less-abrasive-grit emery cloth or use a rubber-bonded abrasive block like the one shown in the middle photo. These are sold under the Sandflex brand name (available at www.woodcraft.com). They come in fine, medium, and coarse grits and do a great job of removing rust from saw tops.

Cleaning

If there's no apparent buildup on the top, you can skip the smoothing part and just clean the top with an abrasive pad like that shown in the bottom photo. Rub a pad across the entire surface of the saw top from front to back and then side to side to clean away any rust or other minor surface imperfections.

Lubricating the top

There are many spray-on saw top sealers available that will seal your freshly cleaned and de-rusted top. Most of these also leave a dry lubricant on the surface that promotes smooth cuts by helping workpieces glide effortlessly on the saw top. The two that we've had the most luck with are Top-Cote and T-9 Boeshield. Both are simply sprayed on the top as shown in the top photo. Allow the sealer to dry completely, and then buff the saw top with a clean, dry cloth. You should see a noticeably higher sheen, and your workpieces will now glide smoothly across the saw top.

Fine-tuning the insert

Since you'll be constantly removing and replacing the insert plate in the saw top, it makes sense to remove any sharp edges that can catch on your hands. Most likely the top edges of the insert are smooth, but those on the bottom aren't. Also, many insert plates don't fit easily into the saw top opening without using force. The solution to both problems is to file the edges of the insert as needed, as shown in the middle photo. If the plate is too tight, file a little and check the fit. Continue like this until it slips into the opening without force.

Because you'll frequently need to insert your fingers in the opening in the saw top, make sure the edges of the casting aren't sharp so they can't tear skin. To prevent this kind of injury, use a small mill file to file the bottom edge all the way around the opening as shown in the bottom photo. Your fingers will appreciate it.

BLADE-TILT MECHANISM

The table top on most scroll saws has built-in stops to lock the table in the most-used positions. At the very minimum, there'll be a stop for 0-degree (straight) cuts; other saws offer stops at 45 degrees or more. Additionally, if you want to be able to rely on the angle indicator on your saw's trunion, you'll need to check it and then adjust it to read true.

Level the table top. To check your blade-tilt mechanism, start by placing a small try square on the table so that it butts up against the blade as shown in the top photo. A small engineer's square works best for this. Loosen the table-tilt lock to just friction-tight, and then adjust the table as necessary for the square to butt up perfectly flush with the blade. Engage the tilt lock to freeze the table in this position.

Check the indicator. Now look under the saw at the indicator as shown in the bottom left photo. If it isn't pointing exactly to 0 degrees, loosen the screw to friction-tight and adjust the pointer until it does; retighten the screw to lock the indicator in place.

Adjusting the stop. All that's left is to adjust the stop. In most cases, you'll find it under the back edge of the table top. Consult your owner's manual for position of the stop and its alignment procedure. The stop is typically held in place with a jam nut as shown in the bottom right photo. Loosen this to just friction-tight with a wrench, and then use another wrench to adjust the stop so it butts up against the underside of the table top. Tighten the jam nut. Now loosen the table-tilt lock and tilt the table away from 0 degrees, and then tilt it back until it hits the stop; engage the tilt lock. Recheck the blade/table relationship with the square to make sure it's right on. If not, readjust the stop. Continue tweaking and checking until the stop halts the table so it's perpendicular to the blade and the indicator reads zero.

Electrical Repairs

A scroll saw's electrical system is simple and straightforward. Power enters through the plug and continues up the electrical cord. On its way to the motor it passes through the on/off switch, which serves to control the flow of electricity. Any of these components can be replaced relatively easily with the manufacturer's replacement part.

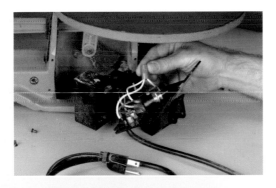

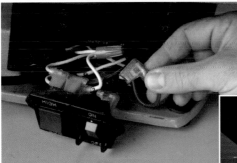

Replacing a cord or switch

How easy or difficult it is to replace an electrical cord depends primarily on the manufacturer of the saw. On some saws you have to flip it over to access the power connections. Other manufacturers offer detachable housings that provide relatively easy access. Regardless of ease of access, once the ends of the cord are in sight, make a note of wire colors, locations, and routing. Replace the cord by removing one wire at a time and installing the matching wire of the new cord, as shown in the top photo. This way you'll eliminate wiring errors.

The complexity of replacing a power switch on a scroll saw will depend on the manufacturer and on the type of switch you're replacing. Switches vary from simple toggle switches to more advanced ones that combine the on/off function with the speed control. To replace a switch, remove the cover plate and gently pull out the switch as shown in the middle photo. Make sure to note the wire colors and locations before removing the old switch. The most reliable way to replace any switch is to disconnect one wire at a time and connect it to the corresponding terminal on the replacement switch.

Replacing a pump

The pump that creates the airflow for the blower of most scroll saws is a simple plastic or rubber diaphragm that sits below or above one of the saw's arms. As the arms move up and down, they compress the diaphragm. If the pump stops functioning, odds are that the diaphragm has lost its seal or is cracked and leaking air. In situations like this, all you need do is order a replacement diaphragm from the manufacturer and replace it as shown in the bottom photo; it should just slip on and off easily. If your saw uses an electric pump to generate airflow, you'll have to order a replacement and follow the manufacturer's installation instructions.

Replacing a fuse

You flip on your saw and there's no power. You check to make sure it's plugged in and there's power to the receptacle. Before you start checking brushes and the motor, check to see if the saw is fused. In many cases, you'll find a small fuse cap near where the power cord enters the motor support or switch box. Pop out the fuse and check it for continuity with a multimeter or continuity tester. If it's blown, purchase an exact replacement and install it as shown in the top photo. If it's good, check your brushes (see below).

Replacing brushes

The motors on many scroll saws are universal motors which have brushes to transfer electrical current to a rotating object (in this case, the armature). One end of the brush is curved to match the diameter of the armature. A spring inserted between the end cap and the brush forces the brush to rub against the armature, causing the brush to wear down over time. As the brushes wear, you may notice a decrease in power. If just one brush goes bad, the motor will stop. Both of these situations call for new brushes; keep in mind that brushes should always be replaced in pairs.

Most saws offer easy access to the brushes via a pair of screw-on caps. Remove these with a screwdriver and carefully pull out the brushes as shown in the middle photo. If the end is scarred, replace it. As to length, replace it if there's less than ¹/₄" of carbon left.

Optical encoding

Don't let the term "optical encoding" scare you. If you've walked into a store and a bell rang to let the clerk know you had entered, you've experienced optical encoding in its most basic form. Typically, a beam of light is shot across a doorway to a receptor on the other side. If the beam of light is broken by a customer's leg, it signals a bell or chime to sound. The speed control on some saws is controlled in a similar manner.

A plastic wheel with evenly spaced holes is attached to the motor (bottom photo). A tiny U-shaped optic device spans the wheel; one side emits light, the other catches it. By counting how many times the beam is interrupted by the holes in the wheel, the electronic controller knows how fast the motor is running. This is how the controller matches motor speed to what you select with the speed dial. If your motor won't change speed, pop off the cover and inspect the optics. Blow out any dust and retest. Sometimes this is all it takes to correct the problem.

INSTALLING A BLOWER KIT

The pump/blower setup on scroll saws will eventually stop working. The plastic tubing gives up the fight and collapses or pinches shut. The diaphragm loses its seal or cracks. Or you have an older saw that doesn't have a built-in blower. Or you're just not satisfied with the performance of the blower on your saw—and many of them do leave something to be desired. Don't be frustrated by dust-covered workpieces where you can't see the kerf for all the dust: Replace the bad parts or upgrade to a new blower kit.

Blower kits usually include an articulated arm, tubing, and plastic cable clamps to attach the tubing to your saw. Air power is supplied by a blower that you purchase separately—the kind used for home aquariums work great for this.

Attach articulated arm. To install a blower kit, start by attaching the articulated arm to the upper arm of your saw with the cable clamps provided, as shown in the top photo. Position the articulated arm such that the blower tip can extend out far enough that it can almost touch the table top. Tighten the cable clamps by pulling on the free ends with a pair of pliers, and then cut off the excess.

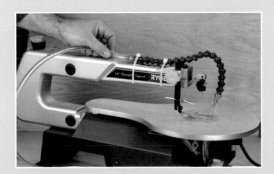

Connect tubing to arm. Next, press one of the free ends of the plastic tubing supplied with the kit onto the nipple on the back end of the articulated arm. A little saliva on the end of the plastic tubing serves as a lubricant to allow the tube to easily slip onto the nipple, as shown in the middle photo.

Connect pump to tubing. All that's left is to connect the free end of the plastic tubing to the aquarium pump that you bought, as shown in the bottom photo. To help the pump operate at peak efficiency, trim off any excess plastic tubing before attaching the tubing to the pump. Plug in the pump, and you're ready to go.

Motor/Drive Maintenance

How often the motor on your scroll saw needs attention depends primarily on what type of motor it is. Small, sealed universal motors need little attention until they burn out. Then they must be replaced. Larger induction motors will benefit from an occasional inspection involving the fan housing and fan, the V-belts, and the pulley alignment (see below).

Keep the motor clean

Both universal and induction motors warm up with use, since all motor windings have some resistance and current flowing through them will generate heat. Larger motors have a small fan blade attached to the nondrive end of the motor shaft to help keep the motor cool. Regardless of whether your saw's motor is exposed or enclosed, sawdust and chips can easily work their way inside. It's a good idea to periodically remove the fan housing and blow out any dust. Dust buildup will add a slight load to the motor and reduce the fan's cooling efficiency.

Check the pulley alignment

If your scroll saw is belt-driven like the one illustrated in the drawing below left, the motor connects to the saw arbor via a V-belt and a set of pulleys. For the saw to run smoothly, the two pulleys must be in line. Not only does this help reduce vibration, but it also prevents excessive wear and tear on the V-belt. To check alignment, position a straightedge so that it touches both edges of the saw arbor pulley as it spans the pulley. If the pulleys are in alignment, the other end of the straightedge will contact both rims of the motor pulley as it spans it; see the detail in the drawing below.

Adjust if necessary

If the pulleys are out of alignment, there are a couple of ways you can adjust them back into alignment. One way is to loosen the setscrew that locks the motor pulley onto the motor shaft and then shift the pulley in or out on the motor shaft until the pulleys are aligned. If there's not enough movement here to bring them into alignment, try loosening the motor mounting bolts and shifting the motor in or out as needed.

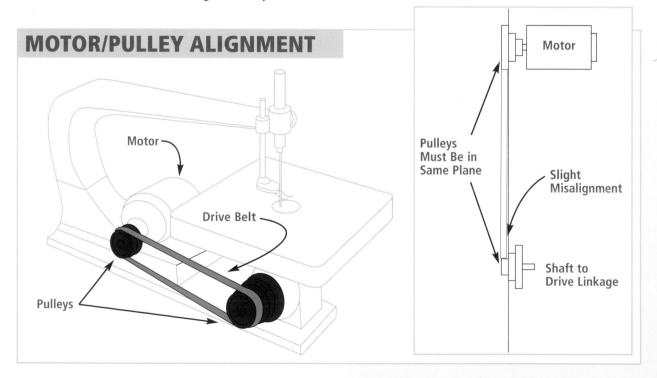

MOTOR/PULLEY ALIGNMENT

Motor

Drive Belt

Pulleys

Pulleys Must Be in Same Plane

Motor

Slight Misalignment

Shaft to Drive Linkage

REPLACING A DRIVE LINK

On most scroll saws, the motor raises and lowers the arms by way of a drive link. One end of this link typically attaches off-center to a pulley attached to the motor; the other end attaches to the lower arm via a sleeve bearing. Because this link goes up and down for every revolution of the motor, there's a lot of wear and tear. Even if you keep it well lubricated (see page 145), the link will eventually develop some slop, and vibration will result. When this happens, it's time to replace the drive link. Depending on your saw, you may want to replace the sleeve bearings at the same time, as they will have worn down along with the link.

Disconnect link from arm. To replace a drive link, start by loosening the bolt that connects the top of the link to the lower arm of the saw, as shown in the top photo. This bolt may thread into the lower arm; but more often than not, it passes through the arm and is held in place with a lock nut. If necessary, use another wrench to hold the lock nut in place as you unscrew the bolt. Pull the bolt completely out and set it and the nut aside. On some saws you'll find a sleeve around the bolt that serves as a simple bearing; set this aside as well.

Disconnect link from pulley. The next step is to disconnect the drive link from the motor pulley, as shown in the middle photo. Here again, the bolt may thread directly into the pulley, but it likely will pass though it and be held in place with a lock nut. Remove the nut and bolt, and if there's a sleeve, set this aside as well. Now's a good time to take a close look at each part. Wipe the part off with a clean cloth and inspect for wear, particularly on the sleeves; replace any that are worn.

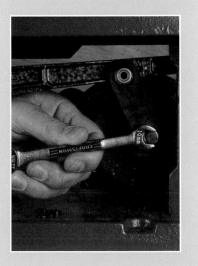

Install the new link. Now you can install the new replacement link. Just reverse the disassembly procedure above to install it as shown in the bottom photo. If the link uses sleeves, apply a few drops of light machine oil to the interior and exterior of the sleeves before installing then. Tighten the lock nuts securely and replace any covers that you removed to access the drive link. Plug in the saw, turn it on, and check to make sure that it runs smoothly.

Maintaining Scroll Saw Blades

Because the teeth are so small and sharpening them is out of the question, there's not a whole lot you can do in terms of maintenance for scroll saw blades. What you can do, though, is to store them properly in a blade holder (like the shop-made version shown on pages 118–119) that keeps them sorted by size and prevents the teeth from rubbing together.

Cleaning

Although you can't sharpen scroll saw blades, you can keep them clean—free from sawdust and pitch buildup. A clean blade cuts more efficiently than a gummed-up blade. The quickest way to clean a scroll saw blade is to scrub it with a small brass brush like the one shown in the top photo. The brass bristles will whisk away dirt and dust without dulling the tiny teeth.

Lubrication

Besides keeping a blade clean, the other thing you can do to help it cut smoothly is to lubricate it. There are numerous spray-on lubricants that do a good job of helping reduce friction as the blade cuts. These are available in pump (as shown in the middle photo) and aerosol forms. Spray a light coat on each side of the blade, and allow it to dry completely before using it.

COLOR CODING FOR SIZES

News flash: Scroll saw blades are tiny—and virtually impossible to tell apart even with a magnifying glass. For scrollers who don't want to use a blade holder (and even for those who do), consider color-coding your blades as to type and size. Nail polish works perfectly for this. You can use different colors for the different types of blades, and a series of stripes to indicate the size.

Use whatever secret code you like, but take care to mark the blade down from the top edge. The last thing you want to do is gum up your blade clamps with nail polish.

Modifying Scroll Saw Blades

One of the nice things about scroll saw blades is that their diminutive size makes it easy to modify them for special situations—something that's almost impossible to do on a larger blade like a table saw blade. There are three basic modifications that you can make to a blade: Grind the ends to reduce the access hole needed for pierced cuts; twist a blade so that you can make cuts in long boards; and hone the back and sides of a blade to let you make tighter-radius turns.

TRIMMING ENDS TO REDUCE ACCESS HOLE

Access Hole

Area to Be Removed

Smaller Access Hole

Standard Blade

Modified Blade

Reducing access hole size

The ends of some blades—particularly small blades like 3/0 and 2/0 sizes—are often wider than the actual cutting portion of the blade. Wider ends mean you have to drill a larger access hole for the blade to pass though for a pierced cut.

This is particularly troublesome when cutting veneer for marquetry, where the larger holes will detract from the overall design. A way to get around this is to reduce the width of the ends by removing some material, as illustrated in the drawing below left.

The quickest way to do this is with an electric grinder. Grip the end of the blade—you only need to do the top end—in a pair of square-nosed pliers like the electrician's pliers shown in the top photo. Press the blade end gently into the rotating wheel to grind away some material. To keep from losing the blade's temper from the heat caused by grinding, stop frequently and dip the end in room-temperature water. Check the end often, and stop as soon as the width of the end matches the width of the blade.

Twisting for long cuts

Occasionally you'll need to scroll a workpiece that's longer than the throat capacity of your scroll saw. When this happens, all you have to do is twist the ends of the blade as shown in the photo at right. Grip the top of the blade with one set of pliers and a bit lower with another set; then, holding one set of pliers still, pivot the other 90

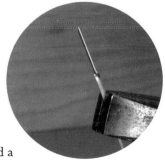

degrees. Repeat this for the opposite end, taking care to align the new "flat" you've just bent into the ends.

Making a long cut

To make a long cut, install the twisted blade in your saw so the teeth are facing to the left or right of the saw. Adjust tension and the blade guard and hold-down, and turn on the saw. Now you can cut a board of any length as long as it's narrower than the throat capacity of your saw, as shown in the top photo.

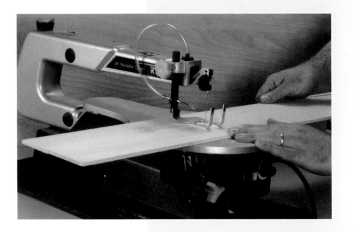

Honing the back and sides

The final blade modification you can make is useful if you're planning on tight-radius turns, or on-the-spot turns. The idea is simple: If you round over the back corners of a blade, this will allow you to make a tighter turn; see the middle drawing.

Honing is easy to do: Just place a small whetstone on edge behind the saw blade and turn on the saw. Make sure the edge of the whetstone is flat on the table top, or else you might end up grinding the back edges at a taper. Press the whetstone gently up against the back corners of the blade to round them over, as shown in the bottom photo. While you're doing this, you may want to hone the sides slightly; see the middle drawing. Experienced scrollers have found that this reduces friction to make scrolling easier. Be careful with honing: It's real easy to contact and dull the sharp edges of the teeth.

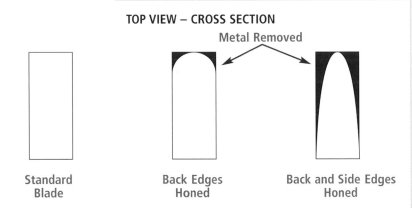

HONING THE BACK & SIDES

TOP VIEW – CROSS SECTION

Metal Removed

Standard Blade

Back Edges Honed

Back and Side Edges Honed

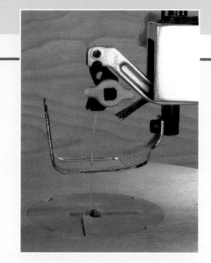

■ TROUBLESHOOTING

EXCESS VIBRATION

Vibration is one of the key causes of scrolling problems. Excess vibration can cause a workpiece to jump and skitter during a cut, can loosen parts, and can cause wear and tear. Here are three common causes of vibration and their solutions.

Blade improperly installed

One of the most common causes of vibration is also very easy to fix—an improperly mounted blade. If a blade is installed so that it's not perfectly vertical—like the one shown in the top photo—the blade-clamping mechanisms won't be aligned and the arms won't be able to pivot up and down smoothly. To keep this from happening, just make sure your blades go in vertical—and stay vertical.

Use an anti-vibration pad

Vibration is very common on bench-top saws because they usually weigh less than floor models and often are just placed on a work surface and turned on. Prevent this by always clamping your bench-top saw to the work surface. Additionally, anti-vibration pads—basically dense rubber mats—can be purchased from most mail-order woodworking suppliers and inserted under the saw as shown in the middle photo. If you haven't tried one of these, you'll be surprised at how effective they are at dampening vibration.

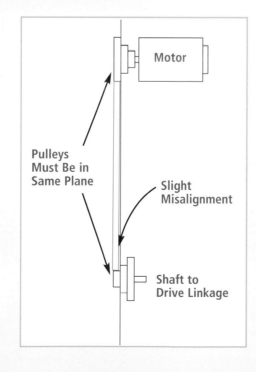

Motor

Pulleys
Must Be in
Same Plane

Slight
Misalignment

Shaft to
Drive Linkage

Check drive-belt alignment

Finally, if you're working with an old saw (or any saw that is belt-driven), vibration can occur if the pulleys of the drive belt are out of alignment, as illustrated in the bottom drawing. See page 154 for more on aligning belts to keep the pulleys from causing vibration.

■ TROUBLESHOOTING

CUT WANDERS

A wandering cut isn't always a huge problem when following a pattern. Often this is solely the result of the operator not guiding the workpiece properly. And mistakes can be remedied by gradually correcting the cut to meet up with the pattern line.

But if you notice that no matter how carefully you guide the workpiece, the cut tends to wander off the line, check to see whether any of the issues below is causing your problem.

Tension is incorrect

A blade that's tensioned insufficiently can bow and flex during a cut. This will be particularly noticeable when cutting woods with well-defined differences in earlywood/latewood growth, such as red oak and white oak. An undertensioned blade will tend to flex and follow the easier-to-cut earlywood. The solution is simply to increase the tension and test the blade by plucking it (top photo) to make sure it doesn't flex much.

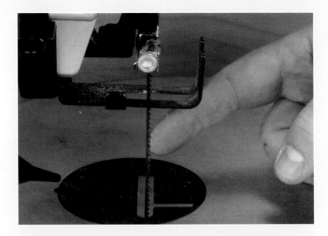

Some blades cause drift

Blades with milled teeth often have a burr on one side of the teeth. The burr tends to grab the workpiece and pull it in one direction or the other. You can test to see whether this "drift" is caused by the blade or not by gently pushing a workpiece into the blade without trying to steer it one way or the other, as shown in the middle photo. If the blade is burred, it will pull the workpiece to one side. When this happens, it's time for a new blade.

Blade is following grain

Even if a blade is tensioned properly and doesn't have a burr, it will still want to take the path of least resistance when cutting. Since the blade can cut earlywood easier than latewood, it'll tend to wander in that direction, as shown in the bottom photo. There's not much you can do about this tendency except to realize it will happen and to stay alert to correct a blade if it wanders off your chosen path.

■ TROUBLESHOOTING

BURNING

Burning is a problem that pops up occasionally when scrolling and can be quite a nuisance. Removing scorched wood from the edge of a workpiece involves scraping or sanding—not something most woodworkers enjoy. Below are three common causes and their remedies.

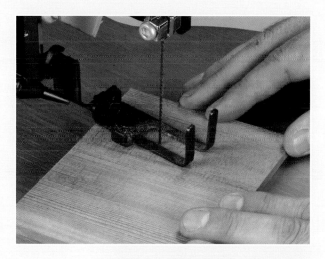

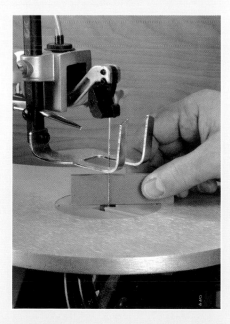

Feed rate too slow

A common cause of burning is using too slow a feed rate. This is especially an issue when cutting thicker wood, where the blade can't effectively clear the sawdust out of the kerf. Built-up sawdust then gets rubbed up and down in the kerf, creating friction that will eventually generate sufficient heat to scorch wood. The slower the feed rate you use, the longer the blade has to generate friction. Two ways to prevent this are to pick up the feed rate, and to use "thick-wood" blades designed specifically for scrolling thicker wood. Thick-wood blades can be found at www.olson.com.

Blade is damaged

Burning is frequently caused by a damaged blade like the one shown in the photo at right. The blade shown here was obviously overheated to the point where the blade lost its tempering. When this happens, the nonhardened teeth will quickly dull and will no longer cut. If the teeth are just rubbing against the wood and not cutting, it won't take long for our old friend friction to generate enough heat to scorch the wood. Whenever you notice that you have to increase feed pressure to cut, it's a sign that the blade has dulled and needs replacing.

Turns are too severe

Finally, burning often results when turns are made too severely. Since most scrollers are interested in making tight-radius turns without burning, it's worth the time to round over the back corners and sides of the blade, as shown in the bottom photo and discussed on page 158. Honing eases the friction-generating sharp corners. This lets you make tight turns without the corners rubbing against the kerf, so wood doesn't burn.

7 Scroll Saw Projects

Soon after most woodworkers buy their first scroll saw, they find themselves incorporating more and more decorative cuts into their projects. That's because a scroll saw lets them add details to a project that they can't do any other way. In fact, there are many fun and enjoyable projects that can be made completely at the scroll saw: intarsia, puzzles, wall plaques, and clocks... the list is endless.

In this chapter, we've included plans and step-by-step directions on how to make eight different projects, ranging from simple puzzles and bookmarks to more challenging projects like a potpourri box and a six-sided night light. But these are just a tiny sample of what you can do with a scroll saw. Once you get scrolling, we're sure you'll catch the bug.

Whether you use the scroll saw to enhance a project by adding decorative cuts to some of the parts, like the shelf brackets and night light shown here, or complete the entire project on the saw, you'll find scrolling an addictive way to spend time in the shop.

Potpourri Box

The problem with most boxes designed to hold potpourri is that they typically contain the fragrance instead of allowing it to flow out into a room. That's because most boxes have solid sides, and the only way the lovely aroma of potpourri can escape is out of the open top of the box. A better idea is to vent the sides for greater airflow—and a richer scent. And as long as you're going to cut vents into the sides of the box, why not make them look good? That's the idea behind the potpourri box we designed; each side features a pierced cut rose, as shown in the top photo. All four sides are identical and can be mitered and beveled as shown here, or simply left rectangular to make a square box; see the exploded view and materials list on page 165.

Miter-cut the ends

To make the potpourri box, begin by cutting the four sides to a width of 3½" and to rough length. Then angle the blade on your table saw to 15 degrees and tilt the head of your miter gauge to 15 degrees. This compound cut will create the angled side box shown here. Cut one end of each side, and then angle the miter gauge 15 degrees in the opposite direction and cut the remaining ends of each of the side pieces to a finished length of 7" as shown in the middle photo.

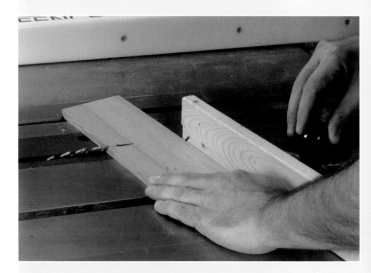

Bevel-rip the bottoms

To allow the bottom edges of the sides to lie flat once assembled, they must be beveled at 15 degrees. Set the blade on your saw for a 15-degree cut, and adjust the rip fence to just trim away the excess, still leaving the width of the sides at 3½". Make a test cut on a scrap piece of wood, and when you are satisfied, bevel-rip the bottom end of each side as shown in the bottom photo.

Attach the pattern

Because each of the sides is identical, you can stack-cut the rose design if desired. This can be difficult with dense hardwoods; but for a softwood (like the redwood we used here), it's easily done. Use spray-on adhesive to mount a rose pattern to two of the side pieces (or individually, if you prefer) as shown in the top photo. If you're planning on stack-cutting, you'll need to temporarily affix pairs of sides together, taking care to align the edges. For ease of scrolling, it's best to apply a strip of double-sided tape to the end of each side. This keeps the tape away from the blade and prevents it from getting gummed up.

POTPOURRI BOX EXPLODED VIEW

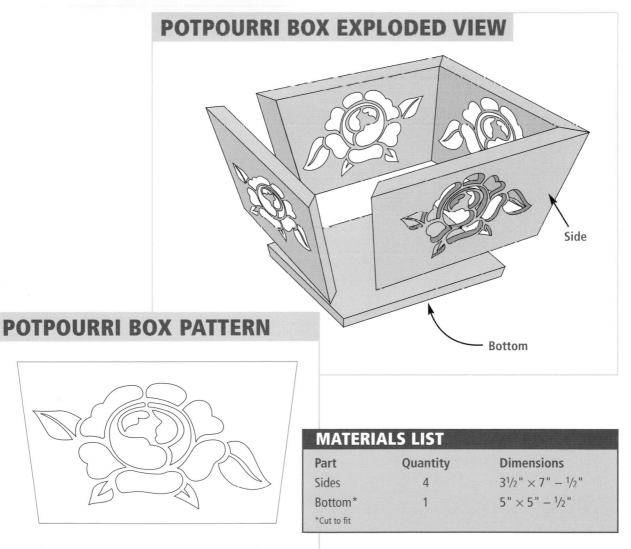

Side

Bottom

POTPOURRI BOX PATTERN

MATERIALS LIST

Part	Quantity	Dimensions
Sides	4	$3^1/_2" \times 7" - ^1/_2"$
Bottom*	1	$5" \times 5" - ^1/_2"$

*Cut to fit

Drill access holes

Once you've got the patterns attached and the sides taped together (if you're making stacked cuts), the next step is to drill the access holes that you'll need for making the pierced cuts as shown in the top photo. Use the guidelines on pages 56–57 to place the holes. Pay particular attention to the top of the rose, where two thin cuts meet to form a tie. The small radii at the ends of the cuts are the best place for the access holes, as this will prevent you from accidentally sawing into and breaking the tie. Since there's plenty of waste area to work with in each of the pierced cuts, drill 1/8"-diameter access holes to make it easy to thread the blade through the workpiece.

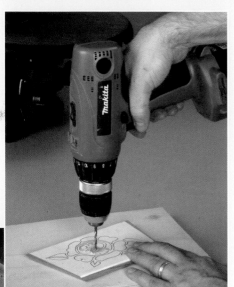

Scroll-cut the pattern

Now you can cut out the pattern. To keep the workpiece as stiff as possible to make cutting easier, start by making the centermost pierced cuts first, as shown in the middle photo. Then gradually work out toward the perimeter as you scroll. When you're done, set the side aside and repeat for the remaining pieces. After they are cut, remove the patterns and separate sides if you stack-cut. If the sides don't want to come apart easily, drizzle a little lacquer thinner between them to dissolve the glue.

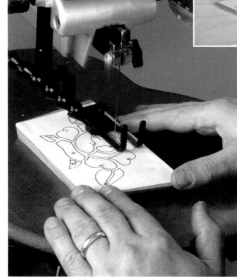

Glue sides together

We used an old boxmaker's trick to glue up the sides. Start by laying out all four sides so their mitered ends are touching and the inside of each piece is facing down. Then apply a piece of duct tape across each joint, making sure to press the ends of the sides tightly together. Now you can "roll" up the sides into box and tape the two loose ends together. Try this without glue first to make sure everything looks good, then unroll the box, apply glue to the beveled ends, and re-roll. Allow the glue to dry overnight.

Bevel-cut the bottom

After the box has dried overnight, all that's left is to add the bottom. This is just a single piece of wood cut to fit inside the box. The edges are beveled to 15 degrees to match the angle of the sides. Measure inside the box and cut a bottom to fit. Then tilt the blade on your table saw to 15 degrees and bevel-cut the bottom.

Attach the bottom

Test the fit of the bottom in the box and trim as needed to achieve a press fit; you don't want to apply any pressure here, as this could crack one or more of the delicate miter joints holding the sides together. Once you've got a good fit, apply glue to all four beveled edges and slide the bottom in place as shown in the middle photo. Allow the glue to dry for an hour or so before proceeding.

Add screen if desired

Although you can use the box once the bottom is in place, you may want to glue some fiberglass screening to the sides inside the box as shown in the bottom photo. This is necessary only if the potpourri that will be placed in the box has small pieces that could possibly fall out of the larger pierced cuts. This is not an issue with most potpourri that uses larger pieces.

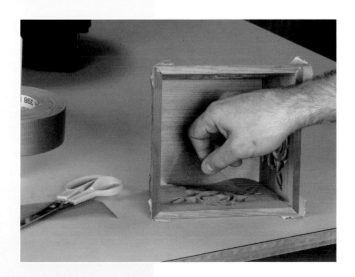

Picture Frame

Picture frames are a lot like clamps—you just can't have too many of them. There's always either a cherished old photo or a new snapshot of the family that would look better framed. You can achieve an interesting effect with a scroll-sawn frame by attaching a contrasting wood behind a pierced-cut face layer, as shown in the top photo. The inspiration for this design came from the teller windows in the U.S. Postal Museum, located in Washington, D.C. You can make the pierced cuts of the pattern shown on the opposite page with precision to closely duplicate the look, or make rougher cuts to create a relaxed Arts & Crafts look (as shown here).

Drill the access holes

Start work on the picture frame by cutting the frame and photo holder to size. Then attach the frame pattern to the frame with rubber cement or spray-on adhesive. Next, drill access holes for all the small pierced cuts and the larger rectangular cuts as shown in the middle photo. Although the drill press is the preferred tool for this as it drills perfectly straight holes, you can also use a portable drill; just remember to slip a backer board under the frame to protect the work surface.

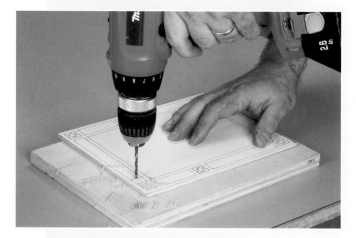

Make the small pierced cuts

Once all the access holes are drilled, you can start scrolling by making all the small pierced cuts in the corners and middle design as shown in the bottom photo. To faithfully duplicate the pattern so the four small cuts in each design create a circle in the center, you'll need a fairly small blade such as a number 5 or 7. Larger blades will make it more difficult to make the on-the-spot turns to create the circles.

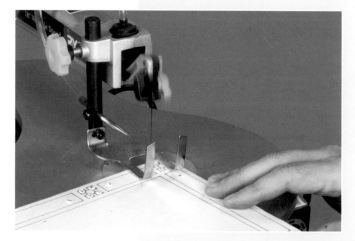

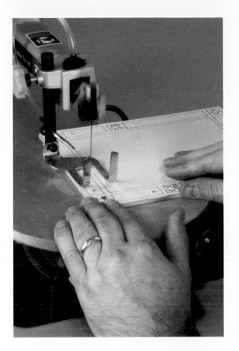

Cut out the larger squares

When you've completed all the small pierced cuts, the next step is to cut out the larger rectangles in the design as shown in the top photo. For the best stability, cut out the rectangles on the ends first, then go back and do the sides. Finally, cut out the large rectangle in the center for the photo.

PICTURE FRAME EXPLODED VIEW

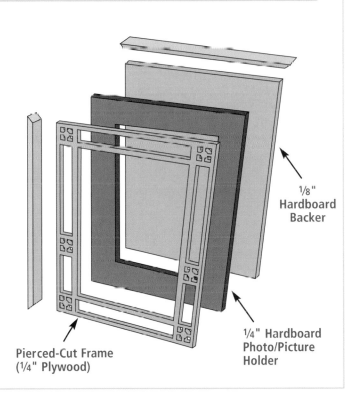

1/8" Hardboard Backer

1/4" Hardboard Photo/Picture Holder

Pierced-Cut Frame (1/4" Plywood)

PICTURE FRAME PATTERN

MATERIALS LIST

Part	Quantity	Dimensions
Frame	1	7" × 9" – 1/4" plywood
Photo holder	1	7" × 9" – 1/4" hardboard
Backer	1	7" × 9" – 1/8" hardboard
Top/bottom molding	2	3/4" × 71/2" – 1/4" hardboard
Side molding	2	3/4" × 91/2" – 1/4" hardboard
Stand Dowels	2	1/4" diameter, 21/4" long

Lay out the photo holder

With the frame complete, you can turn your attention to the photo holder layer, which provides a contrasting background for the frame. You can vary the contrast by using any wood here. Since we wanted a lot of contrast, we used 1/4" hardboard. When finished, this will darken up considerably. To make the holder, start by placing the frame on top of it. Then use a pencil to transfer the inside edges of the frame to the holder, as shown in the top photo.

Cut out the holder

Drill an access hole in the waste center portion of the photo holder, and then cut out the center rectangle of the holder as shown in the middle photo. This is a cut that needs to be fairly accurate to prevent the edge of the holder from sticking out past the frame. With this in mind, it's best to err not on the waste side of the pencil line, but on the other side. Cutting into this side will just cause the frame to extend out past the holder—and that's okay.

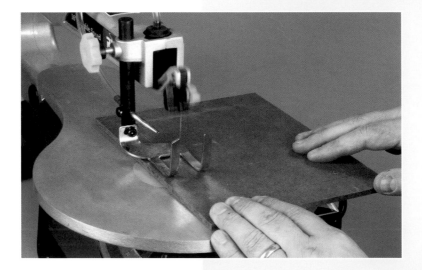

Glue the frame pieces together

After you've cut out the photo holder, you can attach it to the frame. There are a couple ways to glue this in place. One way is to carefully apply glue to the thin webs of the frame. The other is to spray on a couple coats of adhesive; the advantage to spraying is that there won't be any glue squeeze-out. Whichever method you choose, set the frame on the holder and secure it with clamps, as shown in the bottom photo, and allow it to dry overnight (if you used glue).

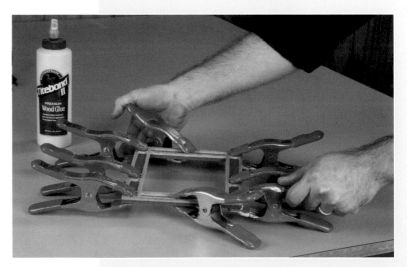

Miter-cut the molding

To conceal the edges of the frame and photo holder, we wrapped the frame with thin molding. The molding strips are $3/4$" wide and $1/4$" thick. These can be cut on the table saw with a zero-clearance insert and a notched sled. Cut the strips long and then miter the ends, working on one strip at a time, as shown in the top photo. For appearance, we routed a slight chamfer on both top edges of each strip. Alternatively, you can cut these by hand with a small block plane, or sand them with a block wrapped with sandpaper.

Attach the molding

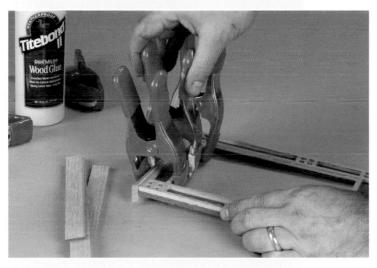

The molding is simply glued and clamped to the edges of the frame so that the back edges of the molding protrude $1/8$" past the edges—this creates a recess for the backer added later. Apply a generous bead of glue to one edge of the frame at a time. Then position a molding strip and secure it with spring clamps as shown in the middle photo. Repeat for the other pieces, working around the perimeter. Allow each strip to dry for a half-hour or so before removing the clamps. Make sure to apply glue to the mitered ends as well, as you add pieces.

Add the back and stand

All that's left is to add the backer and the stand dowels if you're planning on setting the frame on a desk or table. The backer is cut to fit inside the frame (bottom photo) and is held in place with brads or glazier's points. If you want the frame to stand up, you can make a simple stand by drilling a pair of $1/4$" holes for dowels $1/2$" up from bottom and $1 1/4$" in from ends of the backer. Drill the holes through the backer only, and then glue them in place as shown in the inset photo. Slip a photo between the backer and the photo holder, and admire your work.

Night Light

Ever since someone punched holes in a tin can and set a candle inside, night lights have been popular with kids. Granted, punched designs can be interesting, but they're nothing compared to the delightful and whimsical shapes that a scroller can "punch" out of a piece of wood. And what better image for a child to drift off to sleep to than the smiling moon and star design of the night light shown here. Our night light has six sides for 360-degree viewing, but you could also simplify it by just using four panels and square forms; see the exploded view and materials list on the opposite page.

Bevel the panel edges

To make the night light shown here, first cut the panels to width and length. For the panel edges to fit together to form a hexagon, each edge must be bevel-ripped to 30 degrees. Tilt the blade on your table to 30 degrees and position the rip fence so you'll bevel the edge without reducing its width, as shown in the middle photo. Do this for both edges and all six pieces.

Scroll-cut the pattern

With the panels cut to size and beveled, you can scroll-cut the design. We used prefinished 1/4" plywood for the sides, for maximum stability and ease of finishing once the light is complete. Attach a pattern to each piece, or to two or three panels, and tape them together with double-sided tape so you can stack-cut the designs (for more on stacked cuts, see page 79). Drill access holes and scroll from the center out toward the edges, starting with the face profile of the moon, as shown in the bottom photo.

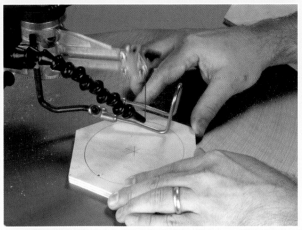

Cut forms to shape

The panels attach to top and bottom hexagon-shaped forms cut from 1/2" plywood. See the sidebar on the bottom of page 174 for step-by-step directions on how to lay out the hexagon shape. Once you've drawn the hexagon on a form, cut it to shape as shown here in the top photo. This is also an excellent opportunity for a stacked cut, as both forms are identical in shape.

NIGHT LIGHT EXPLODED VIEW

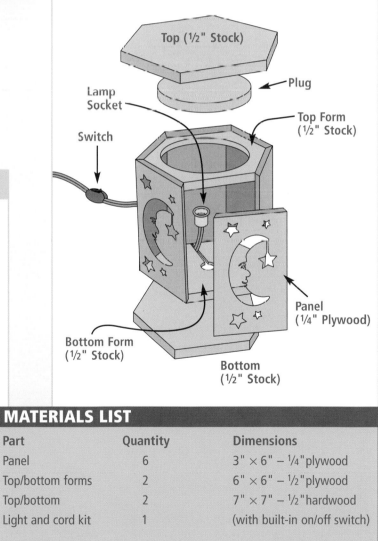

Top (1/2" Stock)

Plug

Lamp Socket

Top Form (1/2" Stock)

Switch

Panel (1/4" Plywood)

Bottom Form (1/2" Stock)

Bottom (1/2" Stock)

NIGHT LIGHT PATTERN

MATERIALS LIST

Part	Quantity	Dimensions
Panel	6	3" × 6" – 1/4"plywood
Top/bottom forms	2	6" × 6" – 1/2"plywood
Top/bottom	2	7" × 7" – 1/2"hardwood
Light and cord kit	1	(with built-in on/off switch)

Cut hole in top form

Once you've cut the top and bottom forms to shape, each form needs a little more attention. A large hole is cut in the top form so you'll be able to reach into the night light and change bulbs. Lay out a 4"-diameter hole and drill a single access hole centered on the marked line. Then carefully cut out the circle as shown in the top photo, and make sure to save the circle cutout—you'll use it later as a plug for the hardwood top.

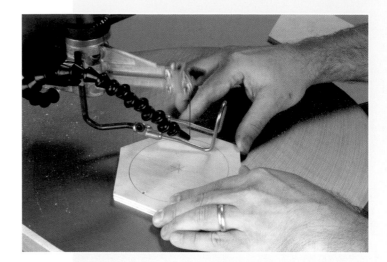

MARKING A HEXAGON

Drawing a hexagon is as easy as 1-2-3. Just draw a circle, tick off the sides, and connect the dots (see the photo sequence below).

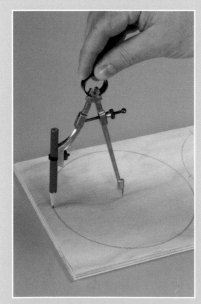

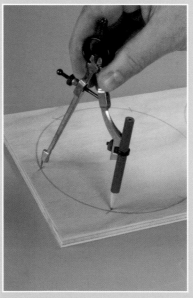

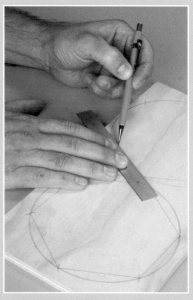

Draw a circle. To lay out a hexagon, start by setting a compass to the desired radius (for the night light forms, this is 5¾", which will create sides that are 2⅞" wide). Mark the center of your blank and draw the circle.

Tick off marks. Without changing the compass, place the compass point anywhere on the circle and "tick" off a mark as shown. Reset the compass point on this mark and make another tick; repeat around the perimeter.

Connect the dots. Now all that's left is to connect the marks you made with the compass. Use a pencil and metal rule to carefully mark lines from mark to mark as shown.

Prepare bottom form

The bottom form requires a bit more work than the top form, as it needs to be cut to accept the lamp. Start by drilling a hole in the center for the lamp holder as shown in the top photo; see the mounting instructions for the recommended diameter. Then mark a $3/16$"-wide slot from the hole to one edge and cut this out on the scroll saw as shown in the inset photo. The groove will hold the lamp cord when the light is assembled.

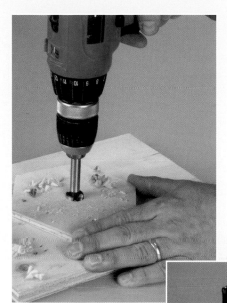

Attach panels to forms

Now that both forms are done, you can attach the panels to them. Before applying any glue, it's a good idea to dry-clamp the panels to the forms to make sure everything fits together snug; trim any panels as needed to get tight joints. Then, working on one panel at a time, apply glue to the edges of the top and bottom forms and clamp a panel in place as shown in the middle photo. Apply glue to the beveled edge and attach the next panel; repeat for the remaining panels and allow the assembly to dry overnight.

Make the top and bottom

While the assembly is drying, you can lay out and cut the top and bottom to size from $1/2$" hardwood. Start by laying out the hexagon shape on the top or bottom as shown in the bottom photo, using the marking procedure described in the sidebar on the bottom of the opposite page. The circle diameter for both of these is 7". Once you've laid out the hexagon, cut out the shape on the scroll saw.

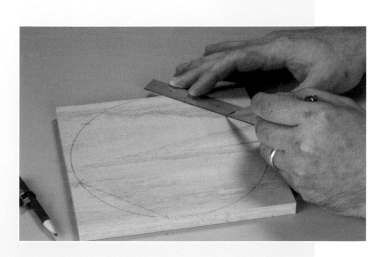

Attach round cutout to top

Pick one of the hardwood hexagons for the top and attach to it the circle cutout you saved when you cut out the top form. This will create a "plug" for the top so it will stay put on top of the night light and still allow you to remove it for bulb changing. Before applying glue, place the circle cutout on the top and measure in from all edges to center the cutout on the top. Mark around this with a pencil, lightly, and then apply glue and clamp the cutout in place as shown in the top photo.

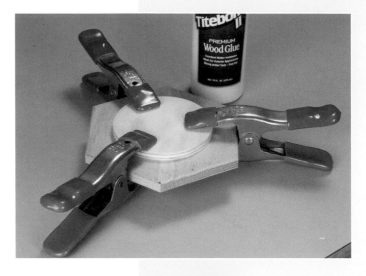

Feed the cord into the bottom form

Before you can feed the cord into the bottom form, you'll need to notch the panel that is attached to the side of the bottom form with the slot in it for the lamp cord. Remove this waste with a chisel, and then thread the cord through the hole in the bottom form so the socket rests in the hole and the cord is pressed into the slot in the bottom form, as shown in the middle photo.

Glue bottom onto assembly

Finally, glue the hardwood bottom onto the bottom form, taking care to match the panel edges with the hexagonal sides of the bottom. Measure in from all edges to make sure the assembly is centered on the bottom. When it is, apply clamps as shown in the bottom photo. Allow this to dry overnight, and then apply the desired finish to the wood. Screw in a lightbulb and press the top in place to complete the night light.

Puzzles

Because of its incredible curve-cutting ability, the scroll saw is the perfect tool for making puzzles. These can be anything from a simple four-piece cutout of a puppy for a toddler, to a complex multi-piece puzzle for a friend. There are two basic methods for making puzzles: One is to cut out pieces and paint or stain them, and the other method is to attach a picture to a piece of wood and then cut out the pieces.

PUZZLE PATTERN

Basic puzzle pattern
One of the nice things about making your own puzzles is that you don't need to follow a pattern if you don't want to. The only requirement is that the parts be interlocking, like those illustrated in the drawing at left.

Cutting a puzzle
To make a puzzle using a picture, start by attaching the picture to your puzzle stock. Poplar, boxwood, and aspen work well for this. The best way to attach the picture is with spray adhesive; 3M's Super 77 spray-on adhesive has an extra-strong hold that is perfect for this. If the puzzle is for a child, consider applying a layer of plastic over the picture to keep it from getting grimy in use. Self-adhesive clear plastic is available wherever office supplies are sold; see the bottom photo. Finally, attach a pattern temporarily and start scrolling (inset). A number 7 reverse-tooth blade will handle most puzzle patterns and leave clean top and bottom edges.

Tongue Drum

The original tongue drums were developed by both the Aztecs and the Africans as a means of communication. Tongues were sawn in the surface of hollow logs and when struck would vibrate, creating a unique tone. The tongue drum shown here is the modern equivalent that can provide hours of fun and enjoyment for kids of all ages. There are two patterns for the drum, both on the bottom of page 180: one for the top to define the tongues, the other for the star-shaped sound holes in the front and back.

Cut the miters

The sides and front and back of the drum are joined together with simple miter joints. To make the drum, start by cutting the sides and front and back to width and length from $1/2$"-thick stock. Then tilt the blade on your table saw to 45 degrees and attach a backer board to the miter gauge to prevent tear-out. Push each workpiece past the blade to miter both ends as shown in the middle photo.

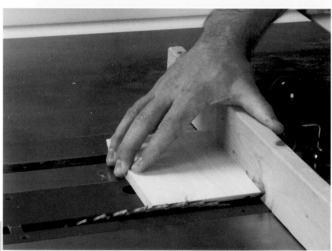

Cut the grooves for the top and bottom

The top and bottom of the drum fit into grooves cut into the sides, front, and back. These grooves are located $1/4$" in from each edge and are $1/4$" wide. You can cut them with a dado blade in a single pass or with a standard blade in two passes. Set the rip fence so it's $1/4$" away from the blade and cut grooves on the inside faces of each piece as shown in the bottom photo.

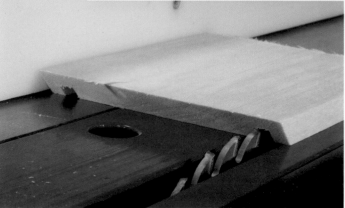

Drill the access holes

Cut the top and bottom to size and then attach the tongue pattern to the top. Also attach the sound hole patterns on the front and back, taking care to center them from top to bottom and from side to side. Once they're in place, go ahead and drill access holes for all the pierced cuts. On the top, drill $1/8$"-diameter holes at the start/end point of each tongue as shown in the top photo. Make sure to slip a backer board under the workpiece before drilling to protect your work surface.

TONGUE DRUM EXPLODED VIEW

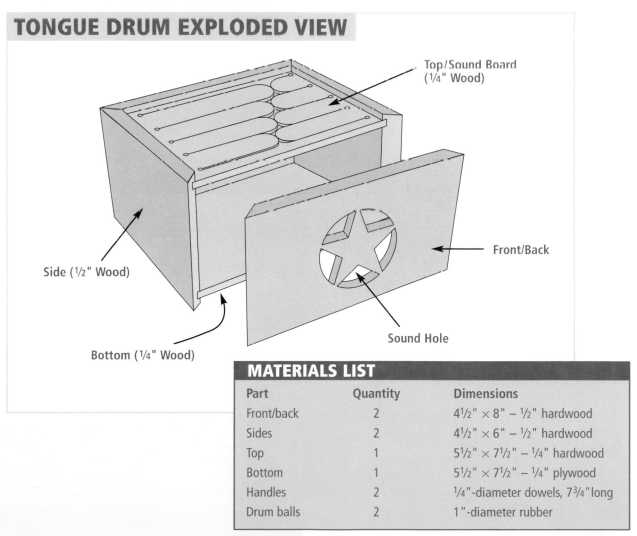

Top/Sound Board ($1/4$" Wood)

Side ($1/2$" Wood)

Bottom ($1/4$" Wood)

Front/Back

Sound Hole

MATERIALS LIST

Part	Quantity	Dimensions
Front/back	2	$4^1/2$" × 8" – $1/2$" hardwood
Sides	2	$4^1/2$" × 6" – $1/2$" hardwood
Top	1	$5^1/2$" × $7^1/2$" – $1/4$" hardwood
Bottom	1	$5^1/2$" × $7^1/2$" – $1/4$" plywood
Handles	2	$1/4$"-diameter dowels, $7^3/4$"long
Drum balls	2	1"-diameter rubber

Cut the tongues

Insert a number 7 reverse-tooth blade in the scroll saw and cut the tongues in the top as shown in the top photo. Thread the blade into one of the start/end holes, and then make a single continuous cut to define the entire tongue. Move to the next start/end hole and cut the next tongue. Repeat for the remaining tongues.

Cut the sound holes

Now you can turn your attention to the sound holes in the front and back. Thread your blade through one of the access holes and make the cut. Take extra care when cutting the corners that define the points of the stars (middle photo) to keep from cutting through the delicate points. Continue threading the blade through access holes until the star has been defined; repeat for the remaining front or back.

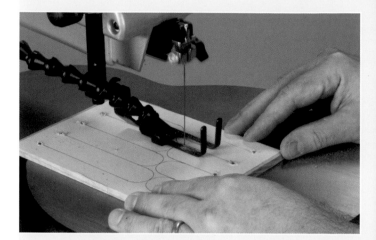

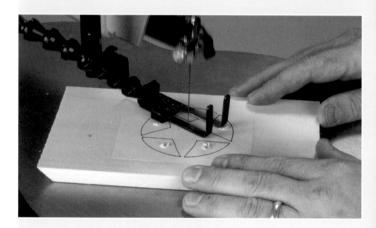

SOUND HOLE PATTERN

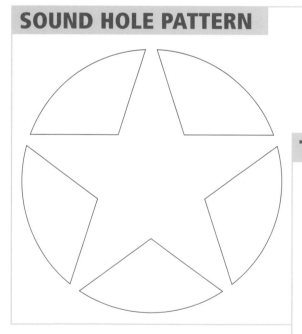

TONGUE DRUM PATTERN

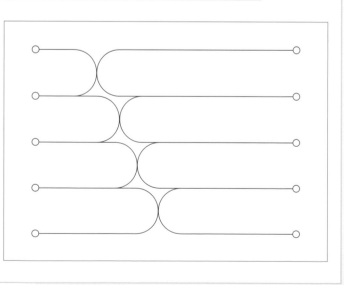

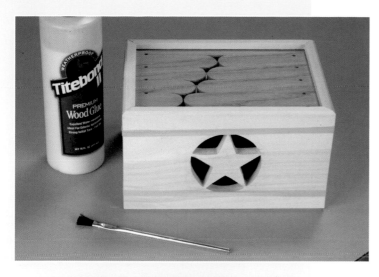

Glue up the drum

With all the patterns scrolled into the parts, it's time to assemble the drum. Before applying glue, take the time to dry-assemble the parts to make sure everything fits together well. If it does, take the drum apart and apply a bead of glue into each of the grooves in the sides, front, and back, and then apply glue to both mitered ends of each part. Slip the top and bottom in place as you assemble the drum. Clamping pressure is easily applied with some stout rubber bands, as shown in the top photo, or with a pair of band clamps. Allow the glue to dry overnight.

Drill holes in the balls

The drumsticks for the drum are nothing more than a couple of rubber bounce balls fitted with wood dowels as handles. To safely drill holes in the balls, hold them with a handscrew (as shown in the middle photo) or other clamp. Drill 1/4"-diameter holes roughly halfway into each ball. Do not use golf balls or any other ball that may have a liquid-filled core under pressure.

Add the handles

All that's left is to add the handles. Cut two 1/4" dowels to a length of 7 3/4"; insert them as shown in the bottom photo. Epoxy is the best glue to keep these in place. Alternatively, you can use wooden balls for the strikers—these will offer a harder, higher tone than the lower, richer tone provided by the rubber balls. Apply two coats of satin polyurethane to the sides, front, back, and bottom of the drum and to the drumsticks. Do not apply finish to the top, as it can seep between the tongues and limit the sound they can produce.

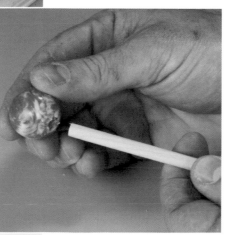

Collapsible Basket

A single continuous bevel cut—that's the secret behind a collapsible basket. Think of the sides of a collapsible basket as the coils of a clay coil basket that you likely made in grade school—except this basket folds flat for convenient storage. What's really nice about a collapsible basket is that it's a very efficient use of wood. The basket shown in the top photo is cut from a single $4^{1}/2" \times 8^{1}/2"$ piece of hardwood. The handle is a bent lamination—thin strips of wood are glued together and bent over a simple form. When dry, it's surprisingly strong.

Angle the table

To make the collapsible basket, begin by attaching the basket pattern to a piece of $^{1}/2"$ thick hardwood that's $4^{1}/2" \times 8^{1}/2"$. Next, tilt the table of your scroll saw to 3 degrees, as shown in the middle photo. As it's much easier to guide the workpiece by starting your cut in the middle of the basket, drill a single small access hole where the cut stops in the center of the basket.

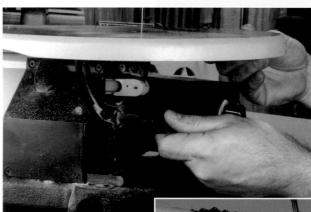

Bevel-cut the basket

Now you can cut the sides of the basket. Thread a number 7 or 9 reverse-tooth blade through the access hole in the center of the basket and start your cut. If possible, try to cut the sides without stopping; just continue to rotate the blank as you go, as shown in the bottom photo. Any hesitation will likely create a bump that will make it difficult to open and close the basket later.

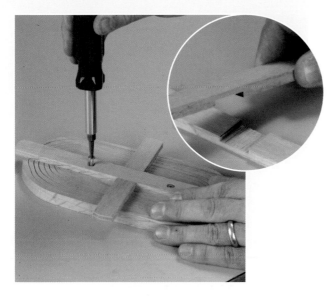

Make and attach the base

Once you've cut out the basket, you can make and attach the base to it. The base is just a pair of ¼"-thick strips that are joined together with a half-lap and screwed to the bottom of the basket. The only one that's really necessary is the short base piece—it provides a leverage point for the handle to press against when the box is opened. Without it, the basket wouldn't stay open. But a single strip on the bottom would cause the basket to wobble, so the long base strip is added to prevent that. Start by cutting the strips to width, and then cut half-lap joints, centered on the length of each, as shown in the inset photo. Glue these two parts together and then fasten them to the bottom of the basket, screwing into the center section as shown in the top photo.

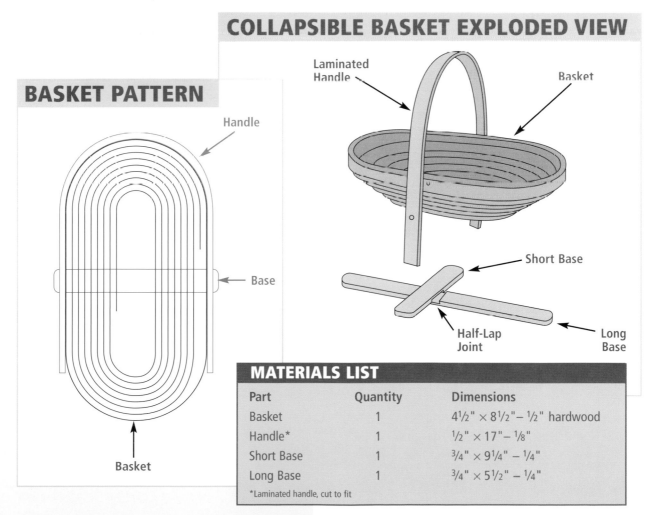

COLLAPSIBLE BASKET EXPLODED VIEW

Laminated Handle

Basket

Short Base

Half-Lap Joint

Long Base

BASKET PATTERN

Handle

Base

Basket

MATERIALS LIST

Part	Quantity	Dimensions
Basket	1	$4\frac{1}{2}" \times 8\frac{1}{2}" - \frac{1}{2}"$ hardwood
Handle*	1	$\frac{1}{2}" \times 17" - \frac{1}{8}"$
Short Base	1	$\frac{3}{4}" \times 9\frac{1}{4}" - \frac{1}{4}"$
Long Base	1	$\frac{3}{4}" \times 5\frac{1}{2}" - \frac{1}{4}"$

*Laminated handle, cut to fit

Glue up the handle

All that's left is to make and attach the handle. The handle is glued up from three $1/16$"-thick strips of matching wood. Cut the strips to a rough length of 20" and then make a bending form. This form is just a $3/4$"-thick piece of scrap with holes drilled in it for clamps. The top radius is 2". Clamp the form in a bench vise, and apply glue to the strips and stack them together. Clamp one end of the strip near the bottom of the form and gently bend the strips around the form, clamping as you go. Allow the handle to dry overnight.

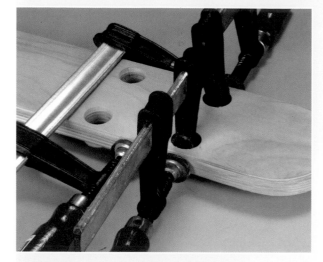

Drill holes in the handle

Once the handle is dry, remove it from the form and smooth the edges of the form as necessary with a block plane. With the basket collapsed and lying flat on your work surface, slide the handle over one end. Mark the center of the basket and then measure 2" out from the center mark. Trim the handle ends to this length. Then transfer the center marks on the basket to the handle. Drill a hole at each mark on each side, centered on the width of the handle, for the screws that attach the handle to the basket as shown in the middle photo.

Attach the handle

Before you can attach the handle to the basket, you'll need to drill holes in the basket for the mounting screws. To do this, you'll have to collapse the basket and then push it out slightly in the opposite direction so you can drill through the outer band of the basket without drilling into inner bands. After you've drilled the two mounting holes, go back and countersink the inside of each hole so the screws will be flush with the wood. Then slip a $1/8$"-diameter brass machine screw through each hole. Slip the handle over the screw and secure it with a brass acorn nut as shown in the bottom photo.

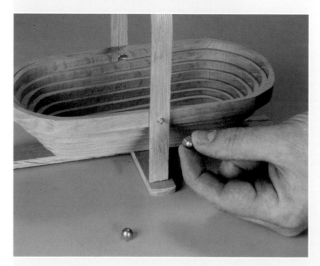

Wall Shelf

When a lot of folks think about scroll saws and scrollwork, the image of a wall shelf with S-brackets comes to mind. There are good reasons for this: Scrolled wall shelves are very attractive, and just about everyone could use more storage space in their house—especially for displaying photos, curios, and knickknacks. The wall shelf we designed is perfect for display in almost any décor. But the real advantage to this shelf is that you can vary the length to suit your needs. Make it short to display a single photo, or longer to show off a collection. And although the scrolled brackets are attractive, the simple curves are quite manageable for a first-time scroller.

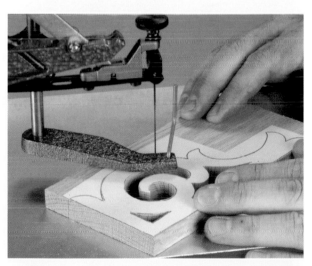

Cut the shelf brackets

To make the wall shelf, first cut the parts to size; see the exploded view and the materials list on page 186. Then attach the pattern to the shelf brackets. Because these curves are so simple and the bracket stock is $1/2$" thick, this is a perfect opportunity to stack-cut the parts. Regardless of whether you're going to cut the brackets one at a time or together, first drill access holes for the pierced cuts. Start by making all the pierced cuts, and then cut the brackets to shape as shown in the middle photo.

Lay out arcs on the shelf

The two front corners of the shelf are notched as a decorative detail. These notches are nothing more than simple arcs. The radius of each arc is $1^1/8$". You can draw these on the corners with a circle template as shown in the bottom photo, or with a compass. Alternatively, you can use any round or oval shape lying around the shop—you can even draw a simple S-curve if you want more detail.

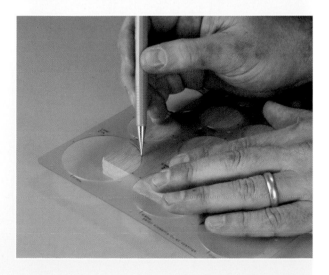

Cut out the arcs

After you've laid out the arcs on the corners of the wall shelf, cut them out on the scroll saw as shown in the top photo. When complete, rout, plane, or sand a ⅛" chamfer on the top and bottom edges of the sides and the front edges of the shelf. Likewise, shape the bottom front edge of the back and the bottom front edge of the support. Note: You can omit the support if you don't mind screws showing in the top of the shelf.

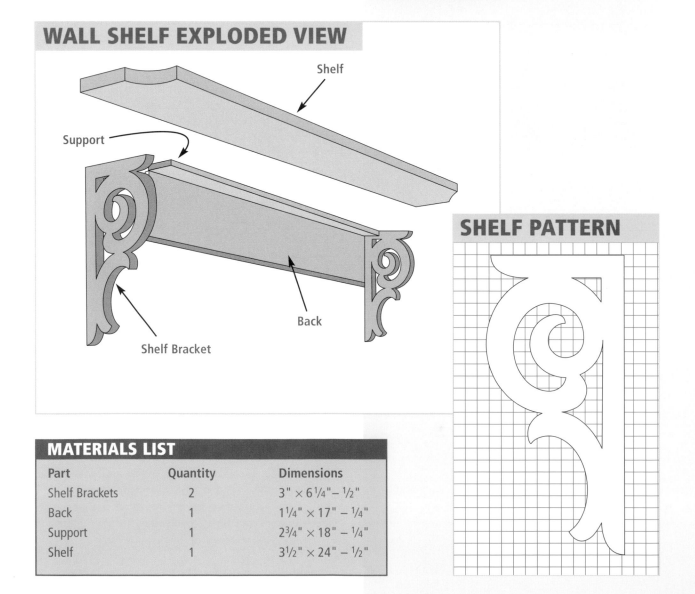

WALL SHELF EXPLODED VIEW

Shelf

Support

Back

Shelf Bracket

SHELF PATTERN

MATERIALS LIST

Part	Quantity	Dimensions
Shelf Brackets	2	3" × 6¼" – ½"
Back	1	1¼" × 17" – ¼"
Support	1	2¾" × 18" – ¼"
Shelf	1	3½" × 24" – ½"

Glue the support to the back

The back and the support are glued together to create a rigid shelf. The support provides a convenient surface for screwing through to attach the shelf to a wall. The brackets are secured to the support with screws and then covered with the shelf to hide the screws. Apply a generous bead of glue to the top edge of the support, and secure it the back so it's centered from side to side, as shown in the top photo. Spring clamps will provide all the clamping power you'll need. Allow the glue to dry for several hours before proceeding.

Attach the brackets

Once the glue on the back and support assembly has dried, the next step is to attach the brackets to the support with screws. Align each bracket so it's flush with the end of the support and drill two pilot holes at each end through the support and into the bracket. Secure the bracket to the support with glue and #6 × 5/8" woodscrews, as shown in the middle photo.

Glue on the shelf

Finally, you can attach the shelf to the support to conceal the screws. Apply an even coat of glue onto the top of the support, and position the shelf on it so it's centered from side to side and has an equal overhang on each end. Clamp the shelf in place with spring clamps, and allow the glue to dry overnight. To mount the shelf, locate the wall studs with an electronic stud finder and drill counterbored holes through the support at these locations. Attach the shelf to the studs with screws, and conceal the mounting holes with matching wood plugs.

Bookmarks

Here's a fun project that everyone will like—a personalized bookmark. There are any number of materials you can use for bookmark stock: thin wood, metal, and even plastic. The flexible plastic we used here is cut from a colored plastic 3-ring binder. This works great, as it's super-flexible and scrolls easily. Use the letter patterns on the opposite page to spell names or just a monogram—or scroll-cut a whimsical design. These are quick gifts to make, especially if you stack-cut a couple for the same person.

Attach the workpiece to a blank

Because thin stock is tough to cut without damage, start by attaching your material of choice with spray-on adhesive to a thin, flat piece of scrap like the $^1\!/_4$" plywood shown in the top photo. If you're using plastic, you may want to consider using an extra-hold adhesive like 3M's Super 77 adhesive. Once you've attached your workpiece to the blank, attach the letters you want to the workpiece so they're centered from side to side and from top to bottom.

Scroll-cut the pattern

If you're going to be scrolling the letters shown on the opposite page, first drill any access holes as needed. Then thread a number 5 reverse-tooth blade through one of the access holes and cut out the letter, as shown in the bottom photo. Continue like this until all the letters are cut out.

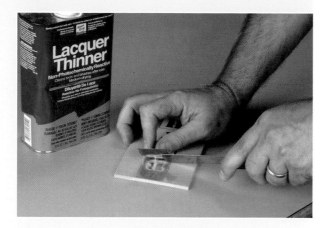

Separate the parts

All that's left is to separate the parts. Because you're working with thin stock here, be very careful pulling the parts apart to keep from damaging them. If either the pattern sticks to the workpiece or the workpiece sticks to the blank, drizzle a little lacquer thinner between them to dissolve the glue and loosen its grip. If you're using plastic, make sure to first test the solvent on a scrap of material to make sure it doesn't cause any damage. Some plastics do not react well to solvents and can cloud over.

LETTER PATTERNS

A B C D E F
G H I J K L M
N O P Q R S
T U V W X Y Z

INDEX

METRIC EQUIVALENCY CHART

Inches to millimeters and centimeters

inches	mm	cm	inches	cm	inches	cm
1/8	3	0.3	9	22.9	30	76.2
1/4	6	0.6	10	25.4	31	78.7
3/8	10	1.0	11	27.9	32	81.3
1/2	13	1.3	12	30.5	33	83.8
5/8	16	1.6	13	33.0	34	86.4
3/4	19	1.9	14	35.6	35	88.9
7/8	22	2.2	15	38.1	36	91.4
1	25	2.5	16	40.6	37	94.0
1 1/4	32	3.2	17	43.2	38	96.5
1 1/2	38	3.8	18	45.7	39	99.1
1 3/4	44	4.4	19	48.3	40	101.6
2	51	5.1	20	50.8	41	104.1
2 1/2	64	6.4	21	53.3	42	106.7
3	76	7.6	22	55.9	43	109.2
3 1/2	89	8.9	23	58.4	44	111.8
4	102	10.2	24	61.0	45	114.3
4 1/2	114	11.4	25	63.5	46	116.8
5	127	12.7	26	66.0	47	119.4
6	152	15.2	27	68.6	48	121.9
7	178	17.8	28	71.1	49	124.5
8	203	20.3	29	73.7	50	127.0

mm = millimeters   cm = centimeters

Scroll Saw book photo credits

Photos courtesy of Bosch Power Tools/Dremel (www.dremel.com): page 11, page 20 (bottom left photo), page 38 (bottom photo), page 39 (bottom photo).

Photo courtesy of DeWalt Tools (www.dewalt.com): page 12.

Photos courtesy of Eclipse Saws: page 3, page 13.

Photo courtesy of Excalibur (www.seyco.com): page 37 (middle photo).

Photo courtesy of Olson Saw Company (www.olsonsaw.com): page 39 (middle photo).

Photo courtesy of Powermatic (www.jettools.com): page 9.

Photo courtesy of RBI Industries (rbiwoodtools.com): page 5.